Innovations in Education:
Their Pros and Cons

Herbert I. Von Haden
Miami University

Jean Marie King
Alachua County, Florida, Schools

Charles A. Jones Publishing Company
Worthington, Ohio

To Vivian and
All Those Just Like Her

Cover Design by Todd Kuyper

 Charles A. Jones Publishing Company, Worthington, Ohio 43085, a division of Wadsworth Publishing Company, Inc.

1 2 3 4 5 6 7 8 9 10 / 75 74 73 72 71

Library of Congress Catalog Card Number: 79-152702

International Standard Book Number: 0-8396-0001-1

Printed in the United States of America

Preface

More than any comparable period of history, the past quarter century has been marked by change and the accelerated rate of change. There are those who believe that education is on the verge of a revolution more basic than any since the invention of the printing press.

Change and innovative practices are essential to achieve the good life, but change may be either good or bad. When basic values and long established ways of doing things are under fire, it is particularly essential to chart a steady course. Imagination must be tempered with wisdom. But neither vested interests, inertia, fear of the unknown, nor insistence on change for the sake of change must be allowed to stand in the way of progress.

We are writing this book for all those who want to improve education. The material should be valuable to young people preparing to be teachers and to teachers in service. Hopefully it will be beneficial to school board members, administrators, and supervisory personnel, who carry special responsibility for charting educational improvement. One of the chief values of the book may be for lay leaders who want ready information to help them weigh the pros and cons of proposed innovations.

Thirty new approaches are included in the volume. Some of them might more properly be called *revivals* rather than *innovations*, but all of them are having an impact on education today and promise to exert increasing influence in the years ahead.

The section for each of the thirty innovations includes:

- A definition of the practice together with brief background and illustrative material.
- Significant components consisting of conditions that are necessary to make the innovation effective.
- Proposed advantages and claims made by the proponents.
- Criticisms of opponents and difficulties to be anticipated.
- A summary assessment of the present status of the innovation.
- A list of a few leaders and places associated with the movement.
- A brief bibliography.

The lists of proposed advantages and criticisms have been compiled from presentations at conferences, readings, informal conversations, class discussions, and reflections of the authors. The arguments for or against an innovative practice may or may not possess validity. Some of them may be quite significant; others may be totally indefensible. All of them, real or perceived, should warrant consideration. They should serve to stimulate further study and help in thoughtful decision-making. Even false impressions and irresponsible objections must be considered and answered if broad support for new practices is to be generated.

Present-day ferment presents exciting opportunities and awesome responsibilities to educators and laymen. We are writing this book to encourage those who are planning education to accept the challenges, to avoid the pitfalls of precipitous action, and to grasp the opportunities for progress.

We are grateful to the graduate students who supplied valuable ideas and helpful suggestions. Appreciation is expressed to colleagues and professional friends who reviewed parts of the manuscript, including Harold Armstrong, D. Louis Christensen, Willard Fox, and F. Joe Crosswhite. Recognition is due the state departments of public instruction and superintendents of schools who supplied materials and names of persons and school systems actively involved in innovative practices. Regretfully, only a few of their valuable contributions could be included in the book.

H. I. Von Haden
Jean Marie King

Note

Suggestions for Using the Material

The volume should be particularly valuable for groups studying the introduction of innovative practices in education and for reviewing programs already in operation. These groups might include:

1. Undergraduate students approaching the completion of their preparation for teaching.
2. Graduate classes examining new developments in teaching and learning.
3. Inservice committees of teachers and administrators studying curriculum improvement.
4. P.T.A.'s, boards of education, and other lay groups exploring ways of improving their schools.
5. Special workshops and seminars devoted to one or more areas of instructional improvement.

Example of a Procedure for Class Use

Let us say the teachers and curriculum leaders of the Bellevue Schools have been studying the desirability of introducing one of the innovative practices into their school system. They are now ready to recommend its adoption to the superintendent of schools. The superintendent has asked that three members of the study group present their case to the board of education. Select:

1. Three members of the class to constitute the committee, headed by the curriculum director, to make the presentation to the board. Have the members prepared to respond to the objections that the board is likely to raise.
2. Five members of the class to represent the five-member board. They should be prepared to bring out information that will enable the board to arrive at an intelligent decision.
3. One member of the class to assume the role of the superintendent of schools. He will present a formal recommendation to the board for its consideration.

Example of a Written Assignment

1. Write the numbers of the *Significant Components* that you would classify as:
   Essential for effective operation________________
   Significant, but not essential________________
   Of minor significance________________

2. Among the *Proposed Advantages*, which do you consider:
   Important advantages________________
   Moderately important________________
   Only of minor importance________________
   Really not an advantage________________

3. Among the *Criticisms and Difficulties*, which do you consider:
   The most significant criticisms________________
   Moderately significant________________
   Weak________________
   Ridiculous or not valid at all________________

4. Write out your own definition of the innovation.

5. With which point or points of the *Summary Assessment* do you agree most strongly?

6. With which point or points of the *Summary Assessment* do you disagree most strongly?

7. If you wanted to read four of the references, which ones would you select?

Contents

Alphabetical List of Topics Included

Accountability
Behavioral Objectives
Collective Negotiations
Community Resources
Community School

Creativity Development
Differentiated Staffing
Extended School Year
Flexible Scheduling
Individualized Instruction

Interaction Analysis
Microteaching
Middle School
Montessori Method
Multi-Media Centers

National Assessment
Nongraded School
Occupational Education
Outdoor Education
Parent-Teacher Conferences

Perceptual-Motor Learning
Performance Contracting
Planning, Programming, Budgeting System (PPBS)
Preschool Education
Programed Learning

Sex Education and Family Living
Simulation
Teacher Aides
Team Teaching
Voucher System

Part One
Individualizing Learning

Individualized Instruction 1

Definition

Ideally, individualized instruction is a procedure which aims at providing a unique program for each child. Because of practical limitations in resources, in the teacher's time and ability, and in the child himself, the ideal perhaps will never be realized. Hence, individualization becomes a compromise in the form of differentiation or diversification. Even if a teacher had only one pupil, he would be unable to identify and diagnose all the child's difficulties and make adequate provisions for them.

The objective of individualization is to take into account all the differences that exist in body chemistry, experiential background, specific interests, purposes, personal needs, and learning skills and styles among children. Having identified these differences, the teacher strives to offer unique learning experiences to provide for this perplexing diversification. This approach is based upon the teacher's total philosophy of education, of children, and of teaching and learning. In reality a teacher cannot be an "individualized" teacher; he can only try to provide optimum conditions for an "individualized" learner. He can guide the student toward the realization of his own ability. The pupil must become involved, experience the excitement, and respond to this involvement. He is a unique and individual learner.

A number of teaching-learning systems have been constructed specifically to take these various factors into account. The American Institute for Research, for example, and the Westinghouse Learning Corporation have their project Program of Learning According to Needs (PLAN) which structures objectives, individualized programs, learning materials and activities, and evaluation procedures. The computer is used extensively. Individually Guided Education (IGE) developed by the Institute for Development of Educational Activities (/I/D/E/A/) consists of four steps in the learning process. These include the diagnosis of the learner's needs, establishment of objectives consistent with these needs, the learning program, and assessment of outcomes. Research for Better Schools has its Individually Prescribed Instruction (IPI). It emphasizes independent work, teacher assistance rather than domination, careful diagnosis, and evaluation of results in terms of individually developed objectives.

Significant Components *Which are essential?*

1. Emerging patterns of instruction should change the primary focus of the classroom from teaching to learning.
2. Student-centered teachers should perceive of themselves as diagnosticians and facilitators of learning.
3. Creative and imaginative teachers are quick to diagnose problems and see ways in which they can provide appropriate help.
4. Materials, including texts, must be plentiful and varied to accommodate a multi-sensory approach.
5. Effective individualization requires small classes.
6. Teacher aides and clerical help enable the teacher to give more special attention to the students.
7. Students should be enabled to engage in learning activities of their own choosing and at their own rate.
8. Rigid standards such as the expectation that children must read in the first grade or spell certain words in the second must be discarded.
9. The immediate objectives of the school work must be precise and clear to both the student and the teacher, and the long-range goals understood by parents and teachers.
10. Flexible schedules facilitate in-depth independent study.
11. Methods of reporting pupil progress must be individualized rather than based on comparisons among students.

12. The student must be allowed to work alone when the need for it is indicated.
13. Provision must be made for retraining teachers and for maintaining communication with the community.

Proposed Advantages — *With which ones do you agree?*

1. Provision for enrichment and remedial work is a natural part of the program.
2. Individualization reduces the tendency to categorize students according to intelligence, socioeconomic status, or other factors.
3. Incentives for self-direction, self-motivation, and self-activity are provided.
4. Individualization takes into account variations in learning styles as well as ability and background.
5. Close association humanizes teaching and learning.
6. Greater enjoyment of work results in a decrease in disciplinary problems.
7. The student may go as far as he can at his own rate.
8. Variable time enhances quality and in-depth study.
9. Doing a better job increases the teacher's satisfaction.
10. Minimizing failure improves the pupil's self-concept.
11. The unique qualities and special talents of each student are more easily recognized.
12. Initiative and creativity are developed.
13. Slow students are seldom discouraged; gifted are rarely bored.
14. Reducing dependence upon the teacher provides for self-motivated learning that may continue throughout life.
15. The student feels that he is important because the teacher is giving him personalized attention.

Criticisms and Difficulties to Be Anticipated — *Do you agree?*

1. No teacher can devote the time and energy necessary to provide a special program for each child.
2. Students are too immature to participate in planning their programs, to work alone, and to evaluate their own progress.
3. Teachers, as a rule, are not genuinely interested in students as isolated individuals, do not understand them, and do not have special ability in diagnosing difficulties and devising ways of overcoming them.

4. Common learnings, unity of purpose, and conformity to standards are likely to be neglected.
5. It is impossible for a teacher to discover how a student really perceives himself, which is basic to diagnosis.
6. Lack of finances makes it impossible to provide the materials and personnel needed to individualize instruction.
7. Flexible schedules and lack of conformity foster disciplinary problems and create general disorder.
8. Mastery takes a back seat to continuous growth.
9. Class size cannot be reduced to the point where individualization can be realistic.
10. Many learning problems exist that mere individualization cannot alter.
11. New approaches such as individualization present new problems, which upset and frustrate students, teachers, administrators, and parents.
12. Nonmotivated students need group activity to spur them on.
13. Textbooks are not geared to individualized instruction.

Summary Assessment

During the past century and a half America has struggled with the problems of providing free public education for all its youth. Attention has often been directed primarily to quantitative considerations. Currently, the chief concern is to assure appropriate education for each youth. Qualitative factors are coming into their own.

The behavioral sciences have demonstrated the broad range of differences in intelligence, special talents, interests, backgrounds, frustrations, and satisfactions that children bring to school. Teachers, too, have recognized the many problems that these multifold variations present in the classroom. Rapid growth in school enrollments and shortage of qualified teachers have, in many quarters, resulted in excessive class size and focused attention on group instruction. However, during the last few years the nation's birth rate has declined, and the supply of teachers has increased. Now hope begins to rise that finally individualization of instruction may advance more rapidly.

Nongrading, team teaching, the middle school, programed learning, use of paraprofessionals, audio-visual aids, cybernetics, better trained teachers all stand ready to advance education through providing unique programs for unique learners. Diagnosis and prescription, the true prerequisites for individualized instruction, may become a reality in the classroom.

A Few Leaders in the Movement

Patricia Anzalone	Madeline Hunter	Edwin Reid
B. Frank Brown	William Kessen	Dona Stahl
John I. Goodlad	William Olsen	J. Lloyd Trump

A Few Places Where the Innovation Is Used

Cypress, Tex.	Haxtun, Colo.	Salt Lake City, Utah
Dayton, Ohio	Janesville, Wis.	San Francisco, Calif.
Decatur, Ga.	Los Angeles, Calif.	Springfield, Ohio
Duluth, Minn.	Melbourne, Fla.	Temple City, Calif.
Evanston, Ill.	Palo Alto, Calif.	Valhalla, N.Y.
Fort Lauderdale, Fla.	Pendleton, Oreg.	Washington, D.C.
Hagerman, Idaho	Philadelphia, Pa.	West Dover, Del.

Bibliography

Arena, John E., "An Instrument for Individualizing Instruction," *Educational Leadership,* XXVII, No. 8 (1970), 784-787.

Baker, Gail L. and Isadore Goldberg, "The Individualized Learning System," *Educational Leadership,* XXVII, No. 8 (1970), 775-780.

Duker, Sam, *Individualized Reading: Readings.* Metuchen, N.J.: Scarecrow Press, 1969.

Flanagan, John C., "Individualizing Education," *Education,* XC, No. 3 (1970), 191-206.

Frazier, Alexander, "Individualized Instruction," *Educational Leadership,* XXV, No. 7 (1968), 616-624.

Goodlad, John I. and M. Frances Klein, *Behind the Classroom Door.* Worthington, Ohio: Charles A. Jones, 1970.

Mitzel, Harold E., "The Impending Instruction Revolution," *Phi Delta Kappan,* LI, No. 8 (1970), 434-439.

Nelson, Henry B., ed., "Individualizing Instruction," *The Sixty-First Yearbook of the National Society for the Study of Education.* Chicago: The National Society for the Study of Education, 1962.

Ogston, Thomas J., "Individualized Instruction: Changing Role of the Teacher," *Audiovisual Instruction,* XIII, No. 3 (1968), 243-248.

Saylor, J. Galen and William M. Alexander, *Curriculum Planning For Modern Schools,* pp. 369-401. New York: Holt, 1966.

Stahl, Dona Kofod and Patricia Murphy Anzalone, *Individualized Teaching in Elementary Schools.* West Nyack, N.Y.: Parker, 1970.

Thomas, George I. and Joseph Crescimbeni, *Individualizing Instruction in the Elementary School.* New York: Random, 1967.

Turnbull, William B., ed., *New Approaches to Individualizing Instruction.* Princeton, N.J.: Educational Testing Service, 1965.

Courtesy Cedar Rapids, Iowa, Community Schools

Multi-Media Centers 2

Definition

A multi-media center is a vast treasure house, a creative workshop, a busy learning laboratory. In the treasure house are exciting materials ranging from books, pictures, slides, filmstrips, models, and transparencies to television broadcasting equipment and computers. In the workshop are production areas with materials and equipment from paint brushes to television cameras for the use of media specialists, teachers, and pupils. In the busy laboratory are children surrounded by all learning opportunities and aids that the financial resources of the school district and the imagination of the teachers can discover, produce, and mobilize to assist pupils with their learning. The complete media concept combines the resources of the library, audio-visual department, workroom, and electronic learning center.

Books, libraries, chalkboards, and other learning aids have been used in schools for centuries; but the years since World War II have been characterized by an expanding technology leading to an explosion of materials, equipment, and concurrent strategies for their effective utilization. As multi-media aids grow in popularity and availability, their presence increases the challenge and opportunities for administrators, teachers, and students.

There are two kinds of multi-media centers. Individual building centers include space, materials, and equipment for the use of teachers and pupils in the learning process. Central, system-wide centers are for curriculum development, inservice improvement of staff, and preparation and distribution of materials and equipment that cannot be provided economically or expeditiously in the individual buildings. Hence, the purposes, personnel, and facilities differ in the two types of centers. In a sense, both are depositories since they keep materials and coordinate their use. But, more significantly, both are dynamic laboratories and service centers for imaginative thinking, creative production, and thoughtful utilization of every conceivable aid to learning.

Significant Components *Which are essential?*

1. It is necessary to prepare the staff in the philosophy of multi-media resources and in skills for effective utilization.
2. System-wide and individual-building centers are needed, both serving distinctly different and yet overlapping and interrelated functions.
3. Easy access to materials avoids having them become "pretty showpieces."
4. Professionals should not waste time charging out materials; children can assume many routine responsibilities.
5. To effect full utilization, school systems should devote funds and planning to workshops and other means of media nstruction for teachers, supervisors, and administrators.
6. Evaluation must include assessment of pupil growth, the materials, and the total media program.
7. Pre-purchase consultation, pre-use examination, viewing, and other experiences with materials and equipment enhance the likelihood of their effective use.
8. Teachers should be brought to feel comfortable in using all types of equipment.
9. Use of aids should be a justifiable part of the instructional program and should be coordinated with it.
10. Special effort should be made to introduce children to materials and their potentialities, to show them how to find materials, and to teach them how to use aids effectively.
11. Teachers should start where they are and with what materials they have and move forward from there.

12. Attention should be given to such matters as size and adequacy of space, light control, ventilation, size and shape of screens, and freedom from competing interferences.
13. In school construction, the media center should be planned as the instructional nerve center of the building.
14. The media center should provide a wide range of well-selected learning aids, easily accessible to all, and a climate which encourages their constant use.
15. Such facilities as workrooms for teachers, space for viewing and listening, and carrels should not be overlooked.
16. Wherever possible, students should be involved in preparing and presenting materials and in other experiences.
17. Special attention must be given to the appropriateness of media for specific instructional purposes and for the various maturity levels of the learners.
18. Obsolete and unused materials should be weeded out.
19. Efficiency should be assured in such matters as management, specifications, purchasing, maintenance, distribution, and designing of facilities.
20. Competent technical, production, and clerical assistants are needed for optimum benefits.
21. The director should have a deep commitment to service.
22. Specialists should work together with the teachers as a team in planning the entire program, in selecting materials, and in carrying out the instruction.

Proposed Advantages *With which ones do you agree?*

1. A variety of media provides vital material for learners of different capacities, interests, and learning styles.
2. Production of materials promotes involvement and learning.
3. The activities of the learning center assist in diagnosis and remediation.
4. Activities add vividness to learning, thus increasing retention.
5. A variety of media lends itself well to instructional systems.
6. Multi-media centers facilitate grouping and individualization.
7. Students are encouraged to assume a greater share of responsibility for their own learning.
8. Exploration, discovery, and decision-making are promoted.
9. Students are helped to avoid overemphasis on verbalism and abstraction by giving reality to experiences.

10. Multi-media materials assist in showing the sequential steps in a developmental process.
11. By presenting new dimensions, the learner is helped to assimilate old information and reinforce concept development.
12. Tactile and other senses are brought into play.
13. "Learning by doing" becomes a reality.
14. Multi-media materials lend themselves well to the inductive method of developing principles.
15. Concrete experience gives meaning, balance, and consistency to generalizations, attitudes, and values.
16. Varied learning activities stimulate high interest, lengthen the attention span, and promote persistent effort.
17. The media specialist is brought into the heart of teaching, where he works closely with teachers and students.
18. Sending materials, viewers, and other playback equipment home helps parents learn and generates support for the efforts of the school.

Criticisms and Difficulties to Be Anticipated *Do you agree?*

1. The facilities of the multi-media center are too costly.
2. Establishing a center usually prevents materials from remaining in the classroom, where they should be.
3. Some teachers resent the interference of specialists.
4. Media people in instruction are out of their field.
5. Competent media personnel cannot be found and cost too much.
6. Multi-media centers are better for training than for educating in its best sense.
7. Media emphasize devices to the neglect of intellectual processes and promote activity for activity's sake.
8. Some teachers expect machines to do their work.
9. Some teachers do not use the materials and equipment.
10. Many materials are inappropriate or of poor quality.
11. Learners are encouraged to stay too long with the concrete.
12. Transfer is obstructed since the specificity of direct experiences gets in the way of abstraction and generalization.
13. An assumption is likely to be made that sensory experience is equally important to learners at all intellectual levels.
14. Abstractions are necessary for creativity and adaptability.
15. Civilization has made more progress through ideas and verbal communication than through manipulation of things.
16. Reality is distorted, and the learner is misled.

17. Some unplanned dimensions of experience in the community may be of more interest, concern, and value to pupils than many of the planned activities.
18. Much time is wasted in getting to the point of a lesson.
19. Learning centers are another name for noisy libraries.
20. Introducing machines is an attempt to replace teachers.

Summary Assessment

The past quarter century has brought phenomenal growth in multi-media materials and equipment, particularly electronic devices. The extension has been both in quantity and sophistication. In education, the multi-media center has begun to tear down the walls of the traditional classroom. The diversity of the materials, their increased accessibility, and their growing appeal have started to revolutionize teaching methods.

Few question the value of well-equipped learning centers for motivating children and individualizing their instruction. Relevance and meaning are added to the verbalism of traditional schooling. Some still fear that the computer and other sophisticated devices may destroy the humanizing value of education. Others are apprehensive lest multi-media developments forestall the expansion of study trips, outdoor education, community projects, and other direct experiences with the resources and problems of the community. They believe that much of the feeling and personal interaction of the real world is lost in the representations of the multi-media center.

However, few schools have actually been deeply involved in working with real problems in the real world. The multi-media center will not constitute retrenching. Its printed materials, real objects, and representations of objects, which can be read, seen, heard, felt, and manipulated, will continue to provide increasingly richer opportunities for learning. Just around the corner, poised with power and potential, stands the computer. Like other learning aids it can be combined with human resources and experiences in the real world to enhance learning, but it is not the answer to all educational problems. Educators must not be misled by its awesome intricacies. Neither should they ignore its untapped potentialities.

A Few Leaders in the Movement

Lucius Butler
Edgar Dale
Ralph Ellsworth
Carlton Erickson
Ruth Erstad
James Page
Neville Pearson
C. Spearman
J. Lloyd Trump

A Few Places Where the Innovation Is Used

Athens, Tenn.	Farmington, Utah	Muskegon, Mich.
Ball State Univ.	Grand Island, Neb.	Owatonna, Minn.
Baton Rouge, La.	Grosse Pointe, Mich.	Rockville, Md.
Bibb County, Ga.	Hattiesburg, Miss.	San Diego, Calif.
Buffalo, N. Y.	Indianapolis, Ind.	Summit, N. J.
Eugene, Oreg.	Lakewood, Ohio	Winnetka, Ill.

Bibliography

Anderson, Vernon, "Service Is the Center," *Educational Leadership*, XXIII, No. 6 (1966), 447-450.

Clark, Patricia, "The Magic of the Learning Center," *California Teachers Association Journal*, LXV, No. 2 (1969), 16-20.

Dale, Edgar, *Audiovisual Methods in Teaching*. New York: Holt, 1969.

Darling, Richard L., et al., "IMC—Library Services," *The Instructor*, LXXVII, No. 3 (1967), 83-94.

Davis, Harold, *Organizing a Learning Center*. Cleveland, Ohio: Educational Research Council of America, 1968.

Erickson, Carlton, W.H., *Administering Instructional Media Programs*. New York: Macmillan, 1968.

Hall, Sedley D., "The Instructional Materials Center," *Elementary School Journal*, LXIV, No. 4 (1964), 210-213.

Neagley, Ross L., N. Dean Evans, and Clarence A. Lynn, Jr., *The School Administrator and Learning Resources*. Englewood Cliffs, N.J.: Prentice-Hall, 1969.

Pearson, Neville P. and Lucius Butler, *Instructional Materials Centers Selected Readings*. Minneapolis, Minn.: Burgess, 1969.

Pula, Fred John and Charles Fagone, *Multi-Media Processes in Education*. Worthington, Ohio: Charles A. Jones, forthcoming.

Ruark, Henry C., "It's IMC for 1963: The Third Year of the Decisive Decade," *Educational Screen and Audiovisual Guide*, XLII, No. 12 (1963), 674-680.

Sylwester, Robert, Jack Middendorf, and Darrel Meinke, "Four Steps to a Learning Center," *The Instructor*, LXXVI, No. 10 (1967), 73-84.

VanderMeer, Abram W., "The Impact of New Materials and Media on Curricular Design," *Educational Technology*, X, No. 4 (1970), 53-57.

Wey, Herbert W., *Handbook for Principals*, pp. 55-60. New York: Schaum, 1966.

Wiman, Raymond V., *Instructional Materials*. Worthington, Ohio: Charles A. Jones, 1972.

Wiman, Raymond and Wesley Meierhenry, eds., *Educational Media: Theory into Practice*. Columbus, Ohio: Merrill, 1969.

The Nongraded School 3

Definition

Nongrading is a philosophy of teaching and learning which recognizes differences among pupils and stresses continuous progress of the individual at his own rate. Grade labels are replaced by flexible groupings that are designed to eliminate retention and skipping of grades. Thus, the pupil's progress is not dependent upon that of others in the room. Provision is made for moving from one learning level to another as performance in the various areas indicates. Readiness, interest, and capacity set the pace for each pupil. He learns that he is the controlling factor in his own learning and is expected to assume increased responsibility for its management. Individualization is the keynote.

The nongraded program is most common in the primary unit, is commonly incorporated in the program of the middle school, and is gaining slow acceptance at the secondary level. It requires flexibility in time schedules, in grouping, and in diagnosis and evaluation. An abundance of material of varying interest and difficulty is essential. Rate of progress of each pupil varies from one subject to another. Many modifications exist under the name of nongradedness. No common pattern has yet emerged, and it appears that no such pattern could serve all situations effectively.

Significant Components — *Which are essential?*

1. Grade levels, grade labels, and grade expectations are discarded.
2. Allowance must be made for varying maturity levels, developmental tasks, and learning rates within a group of pupils and within an individual pupil.
3. Only teachers who possess a philosophy of, and commitment to, nongrading and individualization can succeed in the program.
4. A nongraded teacher must be willing to function as a facilitator of learning rather than as a dispenser of information.
5. Sound principles of the philosophy of education, psychology of learning, and mental and physical development must be dominant in the program.
6. The support of the entire school system, as well as that of the pupils and parents, is necessary.
7. Continuous program revision should be an integral part of the process.
8. A wide variety of materials, both in regard to difficulty and interest, must be available.
9. Flexibility in staff utilization, program scheduling, and grouping of pupils must be provided.
10. Moving pupils from one level or one group to another must be flexible.
11. Dynamic and imaginative supervisory leadership is a prerequisite to success.
12. Sufficient time should be allowed to prepare teachers and administrators, orient the community, secure materials, and plan the organization and sequence of the program in order to insure its success.
13. Opportunity in terms of space and personnel should exist for working with pupils in small groups and on a one-to-one basis.
14. Appropriate procedures must be developed for evaluating progress and reporting it to the children and their parents.
15. It should be recognized that some pupils may learn better than others in a more structured program.

Proposed Advantages — *With which ones do you agree?*

1. A sense of success, confidence, and self-reliance enhances positive development of the self-concept.
2. The elimination of pressures due to boredom and excessive competition reduces many forms of undesirable behavior.

3. The dilemma of whether to promote or retain a pupil at the end of the year is avoided.
4. Because teaching and learning become matters related to a specific child, teachers are likely to work more closely with parents.
5. By progressing at his own rate, the pupil may avoid the damaging effects of failure and repetition.
6. The philosophy moves in the direction of individual diagnosis and prescription.
7. Children who are absent from school for extended periods may resume their work more smoothly and more effectively.
8. The program provides a stimulus for experimentation and the introduction of new and different practices.
9. Improved mental and emotional health is a likely result.
10. Since it is an inherent part of the total operation, special help is no longer a special consideration.
11. Continuous progress eliminates the gaps that occur when pupils miss certain aspects of instruction because of double promotion.
12. The program provides for more careful diagnosis and more adequate counseling in regard to personal as well as academic problems.
13. Pupils develop better attitudes toward school, learning, and their teachers.
14. The problem of different rates of forgetting, particularly during vacation periods, is minimized.
15. There are many social advantages in having children of differing ages and diverse abilities working together.
16. Pupil learning, rather than years spent in school, becomes the basis for assessing progress.
17. The greatest advantage of nongradedness is individualization of teaching and learning and the resultant increased achievement.

Criticisms and Difficulties to Be Anticipated *Do you agree?*

1. Too much time and planning are needed to establish and carry out an effective nongraded program.
2. Children may be unhappy if the changes from group to group are not made smoothly.
3. Because nongrading requires a flexible personality, teacher turnover may increase because of requests for transfer or resignations.
4. Some competent older teachers find it difficult to change their thinking and procedures.

5. Most textbooks are designed for graded programs.
6. Misunderstanding often occurs about philosophy, purposes, procedures, and evaluation.
7. Excessive time may be spent with parents because they have no way to understand the progress of their children.
8. Innovations in general are looked upon with suspicion, especially those as different and as misunderstood as nongrading.
9. Failure to prepare and involve the community will result in confusion and dissatisfaction.
10. The nongraded concept is not feasible at the high school or junior high level, particularly if the elementary levels are not ungraded first.
11. There may be a tendency on the part of teachers to persist in reverting to uniform expectations and standards.
12. It is not certain that improved learning will result.
13. The wide range of needed instructional materials makes the program expensive.
14. Colleges are not training teachers for the program, and experienced personnel is scarce.
15. Transition to a graded system at the end of the nongraded experience may cause difficulty.
16. Serious problems may arise when pupils transfer into or out of the school.
17. Parents may exert pressure to move children to higher levels before they are ready.
18. Teaching teams may break off communication with other teams and become isolated.
19. Pupils will not put forth effort to achieve grade standards because nongrading has no fixed standards.
20. Whether a pupil passes or fails is left entirely to the teacher's judgment.
21. Most nongraded programs merely substitute levels for grades.
22. Increased time will be devoted to diagnosis, record keeping, and reporting.

Summary Assessment

Recent concern about problems of education in the large cities and recognition of the shattered self-image of many nonmotivated children have spurred educators to new approaches. They have turned their attention to exploring the reasons why schools have not reached so many pupils. More adequate recognition of the differences among children, the consequent need for more careful diagnosis, and the realization that more appropriate learning experiences are imperative have led educational leaders to the philosophy of nongradedness. Currently it appears that the program holds promise for enhancing the self-concept of pupils by eliminating continual failure. Some pupils are benefited by having the additional time needed for mastering certain elements, and others are spared the boredom brought about by wasting time waiting for their slower classmates.

Somewhat surprisingly, many teachers report that parents who understand the principles, purposes, and practices involved see great promise of enhanced learning opportunities for their children. Teachers are aware of the additional time they must devote to their work, but appear to receive increased satisfaction from their efforts. Because of the demands of time and effort, the nongraded program requires teachers of great skill and commitment. However, the new approach proposes to raise the self-concept of children beaten down by repeated failure, motivate them to greater effort, and increase their feeling of responsibility for their own learning. If it can contribute to these ends, the price of additional time and effort is indeed low.

A Few Leaders in the Movement

Robert H. Anderson
B. Frank Brown
Jerome Bruner
Ruth Chadwick
Robert DeLozier
Lillian Glogau
John I. Goodlad
Maurie Hillson
Francis Keppel
James Lewis, Jr.
Jimmy Nations
Daniel Purdom
Lee L. Smith
John L. Tewksbury
J. Lloyd Trump

A Few Places Where the Innovation Is Used

Appleton, Wis.
Bellevue, Wash.
Boston, Mass.
Brunswick, Md.
Cedar Falls, Iowa
Cincinnati, Ohio
Covington, Ky.
Des Plaines, Ill.
Essexville, Mich.
Greenville, Tenn.
Joplin, Mo.
Lexington, Ky.
Milwaukee, Wis.
Miranda, Calif.
Newton, Mass.
Park Forest, Ill.
Philadelphia, Pa.
Plainview, N.Y.
Richmond, Va.
Tampa, Fla.
Tipp City, Ohio
Torrence, Calif.
Tucson, Ariz.
Wilmington, Del.

Bibliography

Anderson, Robert H., *Teaching In a World of Change*, pp. 45-70. New York: Harcourt, 1966.

Beggs, David W. and Edward G. Buffie, *Nongraded Schools in Action.* Bloomington, Ind.: Indiana University, 1967.

Brown, B. Frank, *The Appropriate Placement School: A Sophisticated Nongraded Curriculum.* West Nyack, N.Y.: Parker, 1965.

———, *The Nongraded High School.* Englewood Cliffs, N.J.: Prentice-Hall, 1963.

Chadwick, Ruth E., Rose Durham, and Marion Morse, "The Report Card in a Nongraded School," *The National Elementary Principal*, XLVII, No. 3 (1968), 22-28.

Dufay, Frank, *Upgrading the Elementary School.* Englewood Cliffs, N.J.: Prentice-Hall, 1966.

Glogau, Lillian and Murray Fessel, *The Nongraded Primary School.* West Nyack, N.Y.: Parker, 1967.

Goodlad, John I. and Robert H. Anderson, *The Nongraded Elementary School*, rev. ed. New York: Harcourt, 1963.

Guggenheim, Fred and Corinne L. Guggenheim, eds., *New Frontiers in Education*, pp. 206-223. New York: Grune and Stratton, 1966.

Howard, Eugene, Roger W. Bordwell, and Calvin E. Gross, *How to Organize A Nongraded School.* Englewood Cliffs, N.J.: Prentice-Hall, 1966.

Lewis, James, Jr., *A Contemporary Approach to Nongraded Education.* West Nyack, N.Y.: Parker, 1969.

McCarthy, Robert I., *How to Organize and Operate an Ungraded Middle School.* Englewood Cliffs, N.J.: Prentice-Hall, 1967.

Miller, Richard I., ed., *The Nongraded School.* New York: Harper, 1967.

The Nongraded School, Department of Elementary School Principals, National Education Association. Washington, D.C., 1968.

Otto, Henry J., *Nongradedness: An Elementary School Evaluation.* Austin, Tex: University of Texas at Austin, 1969.

Purdom, Daniel M., *Exploring the Nongraded School.* Dayton, Ohio: Institute for Development of Educational Activities, Inc., 1970.

Shuster, Albert H., "Principals and Teachers for Nongraded Schools: Preservice and Inservice Education," *The National Elementary Principal*, XLVII, No. 3 (1968), 10-14.

Smith, Lee L., *A Practical Approach to the Nongraded Elementary School.* West Nyack, N.Y.: Parker, 1968.

Street, David, ed., *Innovations in Mass Education*, pp. 52-90. New York: Wiley, 1969.

Weber, Evelyn, *Early Childhood Education: Perspectives on Change.* Worthington, Ohio: Charles A. Jones, 1970.

Programed Learning 4

Particularly Computer Assisted Instruction

Definition

Programed learning is change in response or behavior brought about through the use of materials and experiences built into a carefully organized sequential system. In the present context, it refers specifically to the utilization of teaching machines, programed texts, and computers.

Perhaps the most promising educational advance of recent years has been the serious concern for individualizing instruction. B.F. Skinner's small, inexpensive teaching machines of the 1950's involved learners in active response as they moved through successive frames of very small steps proceeding from the known to the unknown in a straight-line sequence. Following the linear sequences, Norman Crowder and others developed branching programs, which provide for alternate paths through a course. If the student responds incorrectly, he is shown his error and is returned to the original or alternate frame to correct his answer.

In a few years, programed texts, incorporating the principles of the original machines, virtually replaced teaching machines. Like branching programs, scrambled texts provide the learner with alternative paths. Slides, films, pictures, diagrams, and tape recordings complement the printed material. Small cumulative frames direct the learning sequence. Feedback is provided to guide and motivate pupil response. Both programed texts and teaching machines require student responses, follow a planned sequence, frequently allow learners to move at their own rate, provide feedback, and promote reinforcement of learning through successful response. Programed texts have gained acceptance over teaching machines because of their financial economy and greater flexibility.

It now appears that much of the programed learning of tomorrow will emanate from computer assisted instruction. As in other developing practices, the keynote for using computers for instructional purposes is individualization. The computer takes care of many of the routine functions of the classroom and drill exercises with a high degree of effectiveness. Tutorial systems approximate the interaction of student and teacher, and rapid-fire dialogue for instruction is not beyond the possibilities of future development.

Significant Components *Which are essential?*

1. It must be recognized that even the computer, the most advanced of the devices for programed learning, is only in its early stages of development and must not be expected to do what it presently cannot do.
2. In programing, the description of process must be exact and precise enough to be carried out by a machine.
3. Immediate or delayed feedback concerning the correctness or incorrectness of responses is essential.
4. Provision should be made for following correct responses by positive reinforcement.
5. The programer must understand that his primary responsibility is to serve the learners rather than the computer.
6. Teachers must resist authoritarianism and intolerance on the part of the programer.
7. Every effort should be made to safeguard the worth of the individual.
8. The program should guide the student carefully, but not oppressively.
9. Carefully developed behavioral objectives, including skills and performance levels, must be the basis for programs.
10. Feedback should be provided to teachers and administrators for improving the total operation as well as the learning.
11. The time that students are permitted to use their terminals must be carefully scheduled, and students should be able to operate the terminals easily and efficiently.

12. Classroom teachers must be deeply involved in planning and revising programs and must have extensive inservice training in using programed materials effectively.
13. The materials specialist, curriculum expert, subject specialist, technologist, writer, and programer must work as a team to integrate the total course of study.
14. In writing programs teachers should usually start with very simple exercises involving primarily drill and practice and move forward in a gradual progression.
15. Special effort should be made to relieve teachers of feelings of being threatened.
16. Long and careful study, including orientation of the public, should precede the adoption of programs and the purchase of equipment.

Proposed Advantages *With which ones do you agree?*

1. Programed instruction is the key to a significant breakthrough in improving learning by providing experiences appropriate to the needs of each child.
2. Programing is particularly valuable in coping with problems resulting from acceleration and retardation — categories often most neglected in conventional classrooms.
3. Programed learning takes a big step toward having one teacher for one student.
4. Computer assisted instruction in particular offers high motivation.
5. Programed instruction is well adapted to the utilization of a broad range of new instructional tools.
6. Children's questions and problems are addressed promptly and patiently by computers.
7. In the mind of the child, the computer is fair and free from the threat of personal dislikes and vindictiveness.
8. Programed learning involves students in active response.
9. Programed learning allows the learner to use his own style in solving problems, thereby encouraging inquiry and discovery.
10. Scrambled texts are especially well adapted to the instruction of brighter students.
11. Among the most obvious advantages of programed learning is its value for make-up work and remedial help.
12. Students see their own mistakes and are encouraged to select appropriate materials and make corrections.
13. Results of pupil performance are rapidly fed back to the teacher for analysis.

14. A remote access retrieval center allows students to receive data and instructions at home.
15. The computer is tolerant of failure since a press of a key can start the student over with a clean slate.
16. Understanding the capabilities of the computer stimulates teachers and students to tackle difficult new problems.

Criticisms and Difficulties to Be Anticipated *Do you agree?*

1. If machines take over instruction, people will be dehumanized and human values killed.
2. Programed learning distorts the purpose of true education by its neglect of attitudes and values.
3. The results of programed learning may be extraneous because of errors in programing, which cannot be avoided.
4. Programed learning is effective only as it can be made a matter of logic and science, devoid of emotional intensity.
5. Course content may fall under the control of people with vicious biases, who use programing to brainwash children.
6. Few people are available who understand educational objectives, the psychology of learning, and programing.
7. The cost of equipment is too great for most schools.
8. The time, money, and energy needed for planning, writing, and programing is long, arduous, and out of proportion to the value of the process.
9. The glamor of computer assisted instruction may leave the impression with pupils that other forms of instruction are unimportant.
10. Computer assisted instruction proceeds on the false assumption that the computer can learn for the child. He alone can respond internally and thus learn.
11. Many linear programs of machines and texts are dull and unimaginative, boring to brighter students.
12. The danger exists that programed materials are more of a testing than a teaching device.
13. The art of teaching is perverted through the deliberate effort to make teaching a mechanical science.
14. Commercial interests will exploit schools by producing and marketing inferior programs.
15. Many teachers fear that they will be replaced by the computer.
16. The interaction of human minds is destroyed by the intervention of a machine.

Summary Assessment

Programed texts are recognized as valuable aids to many aspects of teaching and learning. Computer assisted instruction has advanced to the point that major breakthroughs are expected to make it a significant help to schools in the near future. Perhaps upward of 1,000 courses or parts of courses that are already developed form a basis for further growth and improvement. As has been the case in business and industry, new installations are expected to increase at an accelerated rate.

Dramatic reductions in production costs of equipment and in operating expense indicate that the cost for classroom use will decrease substantially. More sophisticated technology and teaching strategies will be developed. The potentialities of the computer seem to be limited primarily by the creativity of those planning its use and by available financial resources to utilize its full capacity.

The teacher will not be replaced, but his role will change significantly. New impetus will be given to increasing professional competence, curriculum development, discovery of new strategies, and better evaluation as the computer delivers and presents material, conducts drills, grades papers, and performs a multitude of routine chores. Those who complain that communication between teacher and student will be impaired might keep in mind that it is not as good now as some teachers would like to believe.

However, it may be important to warn against undeliverable expectations. Progress will be slow. Computer assisted instruction will never be magic. It will not make the work of the teacher easier, but it will provide him with a tool to make his instruction more effective and to make his new professional role more satisfying. As a tool, it will be effective or ineffective to the extent to which the imagination of educators can harness its potential and the degree to which they use it wisely or carelessly.

The chairman of the board of International Business Machines (IBM) warns the master and defends the defenseless computer:

> A computer has no conscience. It feels no passion. It has no life of its own, nor any sense of values. It is neither poet nor philosopher. A computer, in short, is a machine, not a man; a tool, not a tyrant.*

---

*William D. Patterson and Thomas J. Watson, Jr., "Man Over the Machine in League with the Future," *Saturday Review*, L, No. 3 (1967), 74.

A Few Leaders in the Movement

Don L. Bushnell
John Caffrey
Norman A. Crowder
Robert Gagné
Robert Glaser
Albert Hickey
S. L. Pressey
B. F. Skinner
Patrick Suppes

A Few Places Where the Innovation Is Used

Dartmouth College
Deerfield, Ill.
Florida State Univ.
Kansas City, Mo.
Maywood, Ill.
Morehead Univ.
New Orleans, La.
New York, N.Y.
Oak Park, Ill.
Palo Alto, Calif.
Pittsburgh, Pa.
Rome, N.Y.
Saginaw, Mich.
Stanford Univ.
Waterford, Mich.

Bibliography

Apter, Michael I., *The New Technology of Education*. Toronto: Macmillan, 1968.

Banathy, Bela H., *Instructional Systems*. Palo Alto, Calif.: Fearon, 1968.

Bushnell, Don D. and Dwight W. Allen, *The Computer in American Education*. New York: Wiley, 1967.

Calvin, Allen D., ed., *Programmed Instruction—Bold New Venture*. Bloomington, Ind.: Indiana University, 1969.

Computer in Education, Bulletin of the National Association of Secondary School Principals, LIV, No. 343. Washington, D.C., 1970.

Glaser, Robert, ed., *Teaching Machines and Programed Learning*, Vol. II, Washington, D.C.: National Education Association, 1965.

Goodlad, John I., "Learning and Teaching in the Future," *Today's Education*, LVII, No. 2 (1968), 49-51.

Goodlad, John I., John F. O'Toole, Jr., and Louise L. Tyler, *Computers and Information Systems in Education*. New York: Harcourt, 1966.

Green, Edward J., *The Learning Process and Programmed Instruction*. New York: Holt, 1963.

Inlow, Gail M., *The Emergent in Curriculum*, pp. 163-183. New York: Wiley, 1966.

Lange, Phil C., ed., "Programmed Instruction," *The Sixty-Sixth Yearbook of the National Society for the Study of Education*. Chicago: The National Society for the Study of Education, 1967.

Littledale, Harold, ed., "Tell It To The Computer!" *Grade Teacher*, LXXXVII, No. 7 (1970), 108-114.

Oettinger, Anthony G. and Sema Marks, *Run, Computer, Run*. Cambridge, Mass.: Harvard University, 1969.

Thiagarajan, Sivasailam, *The Programing Process: A Practical Guide*. Worthington, Ohio: Charles A. Jones, 1971.

Parent-Teacher Conferences 5

Definition

A parent-teacher conference is a face-to-face meeting of one or more teachers with one or both of a pupil's parents. It is arranged for the purpose of exchanging information about a child so that the teacher, parents, and school as a whole can work together more effectively in furthering the pupil's educational development. This common goal of improvement should provide a basis for free and helpful consideration of any pertinent factors and relationships which might assist in motivating and guiding the child. His home and school life, habits and interests, likes and dislikes, strengths and limitations, frustrations and hopes, should be discussed openly and in a professional atmosphere. His self-concept and his attitude toward and relationship with his parents, other members of the family, teacher, and classmates are vital matters for discussion.

Although the conference is frequently looked upon as a means for the teacher to report progress or lack of it to the parents, it should really be a mutually beneficial exchange. At the conclusion, the teacher should have learned as much from the parents as they have learned from him about the pupil's progress. The conference should provide valuable information about the effectiveness or ineffectiveness of the school's attitudes and program. To be most beneficial, the total development of the child, including his personal as well as his academic growth, should be of mutual concern.

Many teachers find home visitation a very effective way of communicating with parents. Getting into the home allows the teacher to see the personal environment and assess the climate which determines to a great extent what the child brings to the learning situation in the classroom. It enables the teacher to discover family interests and other learning resources that can be related to classroom activities. Parents are often encouraged to take a greater interest in the school life of the child if teachers exhibit a real interest in his home life.

Significant Components — *Which are essential?*

1. To achieve maximum results, teachers should engage in inservice training for conducting conferences.
2. In preparation for the conference the teacher should study the cumulative record of the pupil, gather examples of his work, and review information about the parents and home.
3. A brief list of points to discuss will help move the discussion forward.
4. The pupil should know that a conference is scheduled.
5. The conference should be held in a quiet, private, comfortable place.
6. Some teachers find it effective to hold the meeting in a lounge or conference room, where the teacher is less an authority figure than in his own office or classroom.
7. The conference should open on a friendly, positive note.
8. The prevailing attitude should be that of being of help to each other in contributing to the child's maximum development.
9. Information should be exchanged honestly and confidentially.
10. The teacher should not place parents on the defensive.
11. Sincere interest in the child, courtesy, patience, and kindness should be illustrative of a genuinely professional attitude on the part of the teacher.
12. Arrangements should be made for the parents to see other members of the staff if they so desire.
13. The teacher should summarize the discussion before the conference is closed.
14. Desirable follow-up action that has been agreed upon should be reviewed and clearly understood.

15. Whenever possible, the teacher should pursue suggestions of parents and not make promises that cannot be fulfilled.
16. A subsequent meeting at the school or at the home, letters, or telephone conversations may be agreed upon.
17. A record of the conference should be prepared for the cumulative folder.

Proposed Advantages *With which ones do you agree?*

1. The teacher learns about the child's family and community life, and the parents learn about his school life.
2. Comparison can be made between apparent inconsistencies in attitude or behavior in the child's role as a member of the family and of the class.
3. Goodwill that has been established is likely to generate broader and stronger support for the total school program.
4. Mutual responsibilities of teacher and parents are highlighted.
5. Teachers who visit the home see the child in a setting different from that of the school.
6. Insights gained from home visits will assist teachers in analyzing and interpreting problems and information.
7. The parent-teacher conference, if properly conducted, is one of the most vital and effective tools for diagnosing educational and personal problems.
8. Parents are provided with the opportunity to understand better the role of the school and its philosophy.
9. Parents and teachers gain insight into each other's problems and opportunities.
10. Often interests and activities of the child at home and in school are uncovered that can serve as bases for subsequent conversation between parents and child and teacher and pupil.
11. Frequently parents and teachers learn things about the strengths and weaknesses of the child that they would not discover otherwise.
12. Teachers who are skillful in conferences enhance the status of the teaching profession in the eyes of the public.
13. Through discussions with teachers, parents gain useful knowledge, attitudes, and skills to help them in bringing up their children more effectively.
14. Conferences between parents and teachers often are the beginning of lasting personal friendships.

Criticisms and Difficulties to Be Anticipated *Do you agree?*

1. Parents are often uncomfortable when they come to the school to discuss their children.
2. Teachers lack personal qualities and skill for carrying on an effective exchange.
3. Work schedules, small children at home, and other factors present problems in scheduling conferences.
4. Teachers may be poor listeners or tend to be overcritical.
5. Parents may come to the conference with a generally negative attitude toward education, schools, and teachers.
6. Inadequate preparation is likely to prevent the attainment of positive outcomes.
7. Teachers are particularly challenged when preparing for conferences with parents of children who are not doing well in school.
8. The focus of attention may shift from the child to the shortcomings of the teacher, the inadequacies of the school, or the failures of the parents.
9. Parents may take the attitude that teachers are interested only in academic achievement.
10. "Talking down" to the parents or excessive use of negative comments may render the conference ineffective.
11. Occasionally parents may refuse to respond to an invitation to a conference.
12. Teachers may proceed on the assumption that parents know little about children and their development, or they may assume that parents understand more than they actually do.
13. Failure to respect confidences may prevent success.
14. A pedantic approach or the use of educational jargon by the teacher is likely to bewilder and antagonize parents.
15. If differences in viewpoints arise, the teacher and the parent may not realize that both need to make adjustments.
16. Sometimes parents will try to discuss siblings, other children, or other teachers' treatment of the child.
17. Arguments may result from misunderstanding of the purpose of the meeting or the proper roles of parents and teachers.

Summary Assessment

During recent years, parent-teacher conferences have become a common and widely acclaimed method of reporting to parents and communicating with them. Generally the conferences are held at the school, but many teachers feel that conferences held in the home provide a significant advantage by permitting the teacher to gain deeper insights into the surroundings and social climate in which the child spends most of his time.

Although parent-teacher conferences at the high school level are different from those in the elementary school, similar problems and potential benefits exist. In many high schools, the guidance counselor is the chief liaison between the school and the home. In others, the homeroom teacher performs this vital function. Since he commonly does not have his homeroom student in class, his perspective is somewhat different. General adjustment to school and home, program planning, social relations, and consideration of education beyond the high school take on increased significance. Students, too, look upon conferences between their parents and teachers differently from what they did when they were in the elementary school. Some teachers find it effective to have students present at the conferences.

To promote these exciting outcomes and to help relieve many of the acute problems of youth through closer working relationships between students, parents, and teachers, continued systematic effort toward conference improvement should be encouraged.

Recordings, films, simulation techniques, readings, and discussions are being used extensively to assist teachers in developing an interest in parent-teacher conferences and in improving their skills in conducting them. Most teachers report gratifying results from the time they spend with parents. The interest, concern, and positive response of the parents are frequently sources of encouragement. Equally significant is the help that teachers receive from parental information, which enables them to attack many baffling problems with greater understanding.

After a conference, the development of the "whole child" often takes on new meaning. The understanding and sympathy of the teacher increases; the regard of the parents for the school and teachers is often enhanced. Continued systematic effort directed toward the inservice improvement of teachers should assure that their regard is more often enhanced.

A Few Leaders in the Movement

Linda I. Christiansen   Elliott D. Landau   Herbert W. Wey

A Few Places Where the Innovation Is Used

Burkburnett, Tex.	Hooker, Okla.	Oxford, Ohio
Gilford, N.H.	Indianapolis, Ind.	Racine, Wis.
Greece, N.Y.	McMinville, Oreg.	Seminole, Tex.
Hamilton, Ohio	New Haven, Conn.	Tampa, Fla.

Bibliography

Bailard, Virginia and Ruth Strang, *Parent Teacher Conferences.* New York: McGraw-Hill, 1964.

Caswell, Hollis and Arthur Foshay, *Education in the Elementary Schools,* pp. 404-407. New York: American, 1968.

Cheyney, Frazier, "Tape Recorder and Parent Conferences," *Audiovisual Instructor,* XIV, No. 5 (1969), 82.

Cholden, Harriett, "Making the Most of a Parent Conference," *The Instructor,* LXXVII, No. 7 (1968), 87-88.

Graves, Dorothy, "Getting Ready for a Teacher-Parent Conference," *PTA Magazine,* LXIII, No. 1 (1968), 26-28.

Herman, Barry E., "The Parent-Teacher Conference," *Catholic School Journal,* LXVIII, No. 9 (1968), 43-44.

Le Fevre, Carol, "Face to Face in the Parent-Teacher Conference," *The Elementary School Journal,* LXVIII, No. 8 (1967), 1-8.

Sunley, Robert, *How to Help Your Child in School.* New York: Public Affairs Pamphlet, 1965.

Weaver, Charles, "Parent-Teacher Communication," *Childhood Education,* XLIV, No. 6 (1968), 420-423.

Wey, Herbert W., *Handbook for Principals,* chapter 3, "Conducting Parent-Teacher Conferences." New York: Schaum, 1966.

Part Two
Accountability

Accountability 6

Definition

Accountability is the extent to which an individual or institution is willing and able to stand behind its work or its product and to correct a demonstrated or perceived fault. In public education, it refers to the commitment of teachers, administrators, and board members to being responsible for their performance and answerable for the results of their instructional programs.

Public and private education at all levels is not escaping the dissatisfaction and public criticism that is currently being leveled against almost all institutions. The public clamors for holding presidents, legislators, educators, police, industrial leaders, and army privates accountable. In the minds of many, accountability is not a commitment or deep feeling of responsibility which exists within the individual and directs his behavior. To them it is a prerogative of a consumer or taxpayer to demand proof of effective performance or excellence of a product.

Restless, often disillusioned youth are challenging the relevance of education. Disadvantaged pupils find it impossible to compete with many of their classmates. Citizens in general are deeply concerned about the rapid increase in delinquency, drug addiction, and crime. Many parents are unable to communicate with their children, and those without children are disturbed by the rapid change in values, dress, and conduct of young people. All these phenomena are directly or indirectly associated with education and blamed on the schools. Beleaguered by a multitude of disruptions, many of them beyond their control, many teachers, administrators, and school board members have lost much of their zest for the challenges of educating youth. They appear to be waiting for the storm of dissent and militancy to pass. To many citizens, perhaps, their bewilderment and disillusionment appear as indifference and lack of concern and responsibility.

Since early 1970, accountability has become one of the most discussed topics in education. Perhaps the attention currently being directed to it is long overdue. Certainly those entrusted with a responsibility as costly, vital, and far-reaching as education must possess an abiding sense of responsibility and should welcome all fair and sincere approaches to holding them accountable for their trusteeship, their performance, and the performance of their students. Without education civilization cannot move forward, and without accountability education will wither.

It is encouraging, then, that teacher organizations are holding conferences on accountability, that school board members choose "On Being Accountable" as their convention theme, and that colleges of education are conducting seminars on the subject. Fortunately many recent developments in education are closely related to the concept of accountability and will facilitate its implementation. Most obvious among these are behavioral objectives, national assessment, collective negotiations, performance contracting, PPBS, and the voucher system.

Significant Components — *Which are essential?*

1. Accountability must be directed toward better education for children rather than toward assessing blame.
2. To keep the focus of accountability on improving education, openness, confidence, and mutual respect must prevail among pupils, teachers, administrators, boards of education, and the public.
3. Parents, pupils, and board members, as well as teachers and administrators, should be held accountable for discharging their respective responsibilities.
4. The objectives of the schools must be significant, capable of achievement, and clearly understood so that their attainment can be recognized and assessed.

5. Fear, anxiety, defensiveness, and unjustified assessment of blame must be minimized.
6. Schools should not be held accountable for outcomes that are beyond their control or for which they do not have funds.
7. Deficiencies in performance of students, teachers, and administrators should be looked upon as opportunities for diagnosing problems, determining needs, and planning appropriate positive action.
8. Employees who are incompetent or unwilling to perform effectively should be dealt with kindly, but firmly.
9. Board members and citizens who are not contributing to better education should be held unaccountable.
10. In order to keep accountability in reasonable perspective, all those involved must recognize the importance of children's learning, responsibility for commitment on the part of educators, willingness or reluctance of taxpayers, the complexity of forces that affect the development of children, and the intricate nature of teaching and learning.

Proposed Advantages — *With which ones do you agree?*

1. Accountability will enhance the educational opportunities for students and improve their learning.
2. Accountability will assist in diagnosing deficiencies and needs and give direction to planning for educational improvement.
3. Areas that need additional financial and other resources will be identified, and securing of funds will be facilitated.
4. The teacher's role will change from that of a performer to that of a developer of performance—from presenting material to seeing to it that it is learned.
5. Administrative leadership will be assessed in terms of its contribution to better learning.
6. Parents and pupils will be brought to realize that they too are responsible for the outcomes of education.
7. Educators and boards will be forced to clarify their objectives and assess their efforts in terms of results.
8. Accountability will stimulate a search for better ways of promoting learning, including the use of technological aids.
9. Teachers will place productive effort above filling the class periods with busywork, and students will distinguish between being busy and achieving results.
10. Salaries of teachers and administrators who meet the challenge for improved performance will be enhanced.

11. Teacher education institutions will direct attention to turning out teachers who can do the job rather than those who have fulfilled certification requirements.
12. Legislatures and board members will be held accountable for their performance, and voters will support better education if they are assured of results for their money.

Criticisms and Difficulties to Be Anticipated *Do you agree?*

1. Trying to measure the results of education objectively will further neglect those educational outcomes that are at the root of society's trials by focusing instruction on measurable, often meaningless, minutiae.
2. Faithful teachers and administrators, already discouraged by the failure of the home to discharge its responsibility for bringing up children, will be completely disheartened by being brought to task for deficiencies beyond their control.
3. Meddlers, from the proponents of basic education to social do-gooders, have created a public climate in which sound education is all but impossible and are now trying to blame the schools for their own failures.
4. Many educators are convinced that homes, boards of education, law-enforcement agencies, legislatures, and courts have not given schools the backing needed to do an effective job.
5. Teachers should be responsible to their pupils, not to squabbling power groups, whose demands are often short-term and personal.
6. It is impossible to get the public and educators to sit down together long enough to agree on sound, identifiable, and measurable objectives and outcomes.
7. Many of the most valuable outcomes of education cannot be adequately assessed until the student has been out of school for many years.
8. Insistence upon assigning definite responsibility will retard innovations that stress teamwork and cooperative effort.
9. Schools already know what many of the deficiencies are and how they could be corrected, but sufficient funds are not available to do the job.
10. The attempt to hold board members, administrators, and teachers strictly accountable will cause conflict and strife among people who should work in harmony for better education for all children.

11. The whole accountability movement is being promoted by disgruntled people who are unwilling to support an adequate educational program for children.

Summary Assessment

It is unfortunate that those who saw the need for accountability in education felt it necessary to emphasize this need by insisting that the schools have failed miserably in discharging their responsibility. Although it is difficult for educators openly to oppose a concept as reasonable as accountability for educating children, the emotional reaction of many school people has been that they are being unjustly set upon. This feeling of injustice is particularly offensive and destructive among those who have, through the years, been most responsible and conscientious. To thousands of administrators, board members, and teachers the failure of pupils to achieve in the affective as well as in the cognitive and skill areas has been a matter of deep concern.

Hundreds of thousands of school people may be justified in their view that the unrest and changing values of a society that seems to lack direction, unity of purpose, and commitment to identifiable goals have made it impossible for teachers to achieve as they know they should, and what most citizens expect of them. Thousands of others have contributed to the problem rather than to its solution. It is high time that they be held accountable.

However, society must answer several questions before it can presume to hold its educators accountable. What do we as a society hold dear? What values and attitudes should be taught in the schools? For which areas of the development of youth should the school be responsible? What is the proper relationship of the home, the school, and other agencies to the various components of the total education of youth? What are the most important and immediate concerns? What long-term objectives can be developed and agreed upon? What level of excellence are we willing to support?

If these questions can be answered, goals agreed upon, and resources made available, the schools should welcome accountability. It could help the public and teachers be more responsive to the needs of youth, for it promises not opportunity for learning but the assurance that every child will actually learn.

A Few Leaders in the Movement

Stanley Elam	Willard Fox	Leon Lessinger

Bibliography

Allen, Paul, William Barnes, Jerald Reece, and Wayne Roberson, *Teacher Self-Appraisal: A Way of Looking Over Your Own Shoulder.* Worthington, Ohio: Charles A. Jones, 1970.

Barro, Stephen M., "An Approach to Developing Accountability Measures for the Public Schools," *Phi Delta Kappan,* LII, No. 4 (1970), 196-205.

Cleary, Robert, "Responsibility and Accountability in the American System of Education," *Teachers College Record,* LXVII, No. 6 (1967), 466-470.

Davies, Don, "Come out from under the Ivy," *American Education,* VI, No. 2 (1970), 29-31.

Durstine, Richard M., "An Accountability Information System," *Phi Delta Kappan,* LII, No. 4 (1970), 236-239.

Dyer, Henry S., "Toward Objective Criteria of Professional Accountability in the Schools of New York City," *Phi Delta Kappan,* LII, No. 4 (1970), 206-211.

Elam, Stanley, "The Age of Accountability Dawns in Texarkana," *Phi Delta Kappan,* LI, No. 10 (1970), 509, 511-514.

Elliott, Osborn, ed., "Accountability," *Newsweek,* LXXV, No. 24 (1970), 72.

Fox, Willard, "How 'In' Is Accountable?" *Ohio School Boards Journal,* XIV No. 6 (1970), 5-6.

Gallup, George, "The Public Attitudes toward the Public Schools," *Phi Delta Kappan,* LII, No. 2 (1970), 99-112.

Lessinger, Leon, "Engineering Accountability for Results in Public Education," *Phi Delta Kappan,* LII, No. 4 (1970), 217-225.

Lieberman, Myron, "An Overview of Accountability," *Phi Delta Kappan,* LII, No. 4 (1970), 194-195.

Lopez, Felix M., "Accountability in Education," *Phi Delta Kappan,* LII, No. 4 (1970), 231-235.

Meade, Edward J., Jr., "Accountability and Governance in Public Education," *Education Canada,* IX, No. 1 (1969), 48-51.

Nash, Robert J., "Commitment to Competency: The New Fetishism in Teacher Education," *Phi Delta Kappan,* LII, No. 4 (1970), 240-243.

Phillips, Romeo Eldridge, "Whose Children Shall We Teach?" *Educational Leadership,* XXVII, No. 5 (1970), 471-474.

Raths, Louis E., *Teaching for Learning.* Columbus, Ohio: Merrill, 1969.

Rothstein, Arnold M., "Start Measuring Your School's Effort or Your Public Will Do It for You," *The American School Board Journal,* CLVII, No. 11 (1970), 2, 6.

Schaefer, Carl J., "Accountability: A Sobering Thought," *American Vocational Journal,* XLIV, No. 4 (1969), 21-23.

Underwood, Kenneth E., "Before You Decide to Be 'Accountable,' Make Sure You Know for What," *The American School Board Journal,* CLVIII, No. 3 (1970), 32-33.

Wildavsky, Aaron, "A Program of Accountability for Elementary Schools," *Phi Delta Kappan,* LII, No. 4 (1970), 212-216.

Planning, Programming, Budgeting System (PPBS) 7

Definition

PPBS is an integrated system for providing public administrators and legislative bodies with reliable information for analyzing the quality and quantity of ongoing and proposed programs and for making decisions relating to these programs and their financial support. It is budgeting for program and performance. Costs are analyzed in terms of the achievement of objectives. Recently the term Planning, Programming, Budgeting, Evaluating System has become widely used.

Among the questions which PPBS assists in answering are: What objectives should the schools achieve? How effectively are existing programs achieving them? What are the long-term plans? What resources are needed, and how can they be allocated to best advantage? Are there promising alternative approaches to securing better results? Are the funds the public supplies for schools a good investment? How could the return be improved? What priorities should be established among the goals and programs? Should some activities be eliminated? Which ones should be given greater support? Should taxes be increased? How will additional revenue be spent? What specific benefits will result? Should some of the current responsibility of the schools be turned over to other agencies? Should the schools assume additional functions to fulfill unmet needs? What are they?

The first step in a PPB system is listing what the school system expects to do. The objectives must be stated in clear, precise, and, as far as possible, measurable terms so that they can be used as bases for evaluating the effectiveness of educational activities. The school then proceeds to explore alternatives for achieving its objectives, chooses the most promising and feasible approaches, analyzes its program needs, and allocates resources necessary to carry out learning activities needed to achieve the goals. Evaluation, inherent in PPBS, reveals the extent to which the objectives supported by the allocated resources have been achieved.

Through the consideration of alternatives, the process encourages innovation, personnel involvement, and program improvement. The total educational endeavor must be integrated. The line-item concept of budgeting must be replaced by a new way of thinking and of allocating funds. If for example, $15,000 is budgeted for technical assistants, the budget must show precisely the purpose the expenditure will accomplish. Input is determined as it is needed to produce desired output.

Significant Components — *Which are essential?*

1. Most important in PPBS is a commitment to the approach.
2. A clear, precise statement of measurable objectives is basic to initial planning.
3. PPBS assesses the total program, what ought to be, and the contributions of the individual segments.
4. Program analysis and cost analysis must proceed together, and costs must be grouped according to the job to be done.
5. Projections of programs, resources, needs, and costs should be long-term, perhaps for a five-year period.
6. Alternative ways of accomplishing the goal more effectively and efficiently must be explored.
7. The model must provide for producing and delivering the information necessary for intelligent decision-making.
8. The line-item approach to budgeting must be discarded, and a whole new concept of accounting must be accepted.
9. A flexible five-year plan should be updated annually to modify action in the light of actual experience.
10. Teachers and curriculum specialists must participate in setting objectives, assessing needs, and planning outcomes.
11. Flexibility must be provided so that the system can be adapted to the peculiar needs of an individual district.

12. More productive use of resources, rather than reduction in cost, should be the primary goal of PPBS.
13. Everybody involved must realize that measuring inputs and outputs in education is more complex and difficult than in industry.
14. Inservice training of staff is necessary to increase competence in dealing with the hardware and software of the program.

Proposed Advantages *With which ones do you agree?*

1. PPBS provides administrators and boards of education with data for making decisions, establishing priorities, and allocating resources.
2. The system fosters accountability for assessing the role of the schools, the expenditure of funds, and program performance.
3. Legislative and administrative groups have a basis for choosing from among alternatives.
4. Integrated planning among agencies and among various programs within one agency is facilitated.
5. PPBS provides for conducting public business more economically, effectively, and expeditiously.
6. The system offers a basis for deciding whether a change in output is worth the required change in input.
7. PPBS reduces unnecessary and undesirable pressure on public officials because it demands justification for requests and recommendations.
8. Inherent in the system are suggestions for program improvement through elimination, revision, expansion, or addition.
9. Educators are forced to avoid broad, meaningless, generalizations.
10. PPBS promotes better education and is appealing to classroom teachers because it requires that a budget request or expenditure is made only for the attainment of a worthwhile educational goal.
11. The objectivity of the system builds confidence in administrative and legislative leaders, thereby generating greater support.
12. PPBS allows for making comparisons among various agencies and services, their effectiveness and their cost.
13. Planning of needs and funds is placed on a multi-year basis.
14. PPBS gives direction to the entire educational enterprise by indicating what demands it must be prepared to meet and what resources it will need to achieve its goals.
15. Complex programs are broken down into manageable components.

16. Ineffective programs are identified so that they can be eliminated, thus releasing physical facilities and human resources for redeployment to more fruitful pursuits.
17. Exploring alternatives provides a springboard for imaginative thinking and change.
18. Knowledge of progress promotes professional growth and satisfaction.

Criticisms and Difficulties to Be Anticipated — *Do you agree?*

1. PPBS oversimplifies the complex nature of teaching and learning and the intricacy of the mind and emotional system.
2. Establishing objectives may fall into the hands of demagogues with a distorted view of what education really is.
3. Costing various alternatives implies that the value of these options can be assessed before they are tested.
4. The whole idea of PPBS is built on the premise that the value of education should eventually be measured in terms of monetary output as a return for financial input.
5. Although PPBS is designed to reduce costs, it actually increases them substantially because most schools do not have the trained personnel and equipment necessary to implement an effective systems approach.
6. PPBS discourages experimentation, which by its very nature cannot be expected to yield immediate returns.
7. Most educational activities are designed to produce long-term results, not measurable in their intermediate stages.
8. PPBS is a ritual designed to fool the public into believing that their tax dollars are being spent prudently.
9. It is ridiculous, for example, to attempt to determine to what objectives the cost of the multi-media center should be charged.
10. Since budgeting takes place in a political environment, many administrators and boards may resist public scrutiny of all their operations, and conflict with political pressures of vested interests must be expected.
11. Assuming that PPBS can be established simply by putting new categories into the traditional budget is a serious pitfall.
12. It is impossible to determine which school activities are responsible for which outcomes.
13. In too many instances, those who institute innovations are the same people who supply data for evaluating them.

Summary Assessment

As the demand for public services and for revenue to support them continues, with apparently no end in sight, citizens everywhere are beginning to give serious thought to establishing priorities and to holding public agencies accountable for their performance. National defense, health services, social security, education, welfare, transportation, public housing, and control of drug addiction, crime, and pollution compete for the tax dollar.

Currently, next to national defense, public education claims the largest share of total tax revenue. Because of the benefits that accrue to a society from the development of its human resources, the massive funding for education has appeared to be a good investment. However, in recent years, taxpayers have exhibited growing resistence to what seems to be an endless increase in demands and costs of education. They have begun to question the programs and practices of the schools. They have talked more and more about the school's accountability for performance.

Increasingly, budgeting practices have been examined. Many questions have arisen. What are the purposes and goals of public education? Is education taking on too much? How much of the various services do we want and can we afford? Are the schools performing as well as they should? Will the demand for more money ever stop? Would smaller appropriations show any decline in educational achievement?

At the present time, thousands of school systems throughout the country use some aspects of PPBS, although full utilization of the program is growing slowly and resistence to it continues among many educators. It is a valuable tool for improving decision-making. The system facilitates better choices and decisions by providing factual data about plans, programs, needs, resources, and performance. It requires long-term planning, encourages accountability, and generates public support. As ways of determining the relationship between input and output are refined, PPBS will become more pertinent and valuable. It may not reduce costs, but it should increase the effectiveness of educational programs. It forces teachers, administrators, and school boards to rethink their objectives critically, to redirect their efforts, and to evaluate their results in terms of their goals. Reason demands that educators give serious attention to the promising possibilities of PPBS for integrating efficient operation with effective performance.

A Few Leaders in the Movement

William H. Curtis	R. N. McLean	Charles C. Poindexter
Harry J. Hartley	Edgar Morphet	Charles Ryan
H. Thomas James	John Pagen	Allen Schick

A Few Places Where the Innovation Is Used

Clark County, Nev.	Hyde Park, N.Y.	Pearl River, N.Y.
Dade County, Fla.	Milford, N.H.	Peoria, Ill.
Darien, Conn.	Milwaukee, Wis.	Skokie, Ill.
Davidson County, Tenn.	Montgomery County, Md.	Westport, Conn.

Bibliography

Baynham, Dorsey, "PPBS and Several Good Reasons It Shouldn't Scare You Off," *American School Board Journal*, CLVIII, No. 2 (1970), 27-29.

Buskin, Martin, "PPBS Means Better Money Management," *School Management*, XIII, No. 11 (1969), 64-68, 80-82.

Curtis, William H., "Program Budgeting Design For Schools Unveiled, With Much Work Still to Go," *Nation's Schools*, LXXIV, No. 5 (1969), 40-42.

Drew, Elizabeth B., "HEW Grapple with PPBS," *The Public Interest*, No. 8 (1967), 9-27.

Greenhouse, Samuel M., "The Planning-Programming-Budgeting System: Rationale, Language, and Idea-Relationships," *Public Administration Review*, XXV, No. 4 (1966), 271-277.

Hartley, Harry J., *Educational Planning, Programming, Budgeting*. Englewood Cliffs, N.J.: Prentice-Hall, 1968.

———, "Limitations of Systems Analysis," *Phi Delta Kappan*, L, No. 9 (1969), 515-519.

Lutz, Frank W., *Toward Improved Urban Education*. Worthington, Ohio: Charles A. Jones, 1970.

Lyden, Fremont J. and Ernest G. Miller, eds., *Planning, Programming, Budgeting: A Systems Approach to Management*. Chicago: Markham, 1967.

Morphet, Edgar L. and Charles O. Ryan, eds., *A Report of Designing Education for the Future: An Eight-State Project*. New York: Citation, 1967, 266-290.

Planning for Educational Development in a Planning, Programming, Budgeting System, National Education Association Committee on Finance. Washington, D.C., 1968.

Poindexter, Charles C., "Planning-Programming-Budgeting Systems For Education," *High School Journal*, LII, No. 4 (1969), 206-217.

Schick, Allen, "Planning-Programming-Budgeting System: A Symposium," *Public Administrative Review*, XXV, No. 4 (1969), 243-258.

What Is A Programming, Planning, Budgeting System?, National Education Association, Research Bulletin 46. Washington, D.C., 1968.

Behavioral Objectives 8

Definition

A behavioral objective is an observable criterion of performance. It is a clear, precise statement of the student's behavior that will be accepted as evidence of his having achieved what he and the teacher set out to accomplish. It is a goal indicating a task which the student is expected to perform, a way in which he should respond, or a skill which he can demonstrate after certain learning experiences. The statement of the proposed outcomes is precise and describes in unambiguous terms the kind of behavior and level of proficiency that is expected.

In a sense, the term *behavioral objective* is unfortunate. For many teachers it carries the implication that all desirable outcomes of instruction must result in demonstrable overt behavior and be subject to precise quantitative measurement. Hence many teachers consider behavioral objectives quite appropriate for psychomotor learning, but less applicable to the cognitive area and inappropriate for affective learning. Learning should be looked upon as the process of achieving changed ways of responding in cognitive and affective as well as in psychomotor behavior.

These objectives requiring outcomes that demonstrate observably improved performance replace such general terms as *knows, enjoys, understands*, and *appreciates* with such terms as *lists*, *constructs*, *correctly names*, and *selects*. A distinction is made between general objectives, or goal statements, and precise behavioral objectives.

A general objective might be: To develop deeper understanding and appreciation of the thought and style of William Wordsworth. Stated in behavioral terms, the objective might be: Given sixteen two-line selections of poetry — four from Shakespeare, four from Tennyson, four from Milton, and four from Wordsworth — and asked to select the four passages written by Wordsworth, the student should correctly identify at least three of the four selections from Wordsworth and misidentify not more than one passage. If the student is able to present this evidence, both he and the teacher will know that he has achieved the acceptable level of performance to demonstrate his understanding and appreciation of the thought and style of Wordsworth.

Significant Components *Which are essential?*

1. Objectives must be precise statements of specific goals.
2. Objectives must be stated in such terms that their attainment can be identified in observable performance.
3. In order to give substance and direction to teaching and learning, the objectives should state what the student will do after completing the learning activities.
4. Objectives must be based on the needs of the pupils and society and consistent with a sound philosophy of education.
5. Teachers and other staff members of each school must develop their own objectives.
6. Pretesting performance is highly desirable so that the teacher can adjust his original objectives.
7. If pretests show that a student can already perform at the level stated in the objective, the goal should be revised upward. If certain originally assumed behavior is absent, the standard should be lowered.
8. The teacher must develop proficiency in applying sound principles of learning.
9. The established objectives must be worthwhile in the eyes of the learner and attainable for him, and he must find satisfaction in having achieved them.
10. The learner must see a relationship between assigned exercises and the attainment of the behavioral objective.
11. The objectives must be stated clearly and precisely enough to be meaningful and readily understood and communicated.

12. The lowest level of acceptable performance must be indicated.
13. When appropriate, time limits and other conditions should be stated.

Proposed Advantages *With which ones do you agree?*

1. Behavioral objectives serve as the basis for justifying and establishing a relevant program of measurable quality.
2. Behavioral objectives are essential for curriculum planning, program revision, and meaningful evaluation.
3. Behavioral objectives may be written up for affective, psychomotor, and cognitive learning programs.
4. When learning is expressed in behavioral terms, it takes on meaning and clarity and can be communicated to all those involved in the educational process.
5. By telling the learner how he is expected to behave, behavioral objectives suggest to him what to do, how to go about doing it, and what to use to accomplish his ends.
6. Behavioral objectives are a great aid to objective research.
7. Behavioral objectives are a guide for the teacher by telling him whether or not certain strategies and activities are leading in the right direction.
8. Behavioral objectives give significance to an assignment and provide motivation by making knowledge of progress available to the learner.
9. Appropriate objectives will insure success; observable success will stimulate interest and build confidence; interest and confidence will generate increased effort and learning.
10. The teacher is enabled to evaluate and report with greater certainty and assurance.
11. Behavioral objectives help the students in diagnosing deficiencies and in planning further study.
12. Specific, clearly stated objectives are more easily and meaningfully revised than vague, general ones.
13. Aid in the selection of appropriate subject matter, materials, methods, and equipment is provided.
14. Behavioral objectives assist the teacher in self-evaluation and facilitate discussion between teacher and supervisor.
15. Behavioral objectives point out that the cognitive is often overemphasized to the neglect of the affective and psychomotor.
16. Behavioral objectives demonstrate that the attainment of knowledge as a goal is defensible; but that it is only a base for higher levels of analysis, synthesis, and understanding.

17. Behavorial objectives assist in differentiating among different levels of difficulty and quality in various tasks and performances.
18. Behavioral objectives give focus to teaching and learning.

Criticisms and Difficulties to Be Anticipated *Do you agree?*

1. It may be difficult, and indeed awkward and frustrating, to express certain desired outcomes in precise behavioral terms.
2. Outcomes that are easily described and measured are often unimportant.
3. Undue emphasis on behavioral objectives may lead to neglect of broad concepts, principles, and the understandings that give meaning to behavior.
4. Behavioral objectives may focus attention on parts of wholes, minutiae, and trivia to the detriment of integration and unity.
5. Insistence on defining objectives in behavioral terms may invite neglect of affective teaching and learning.
6. Emphasis on behavior may overlook the reasons underlying it.
7. Overemphasis on behavioral outcomes may neglect the development of improved thinking processes and stress the quantitative to the neglect of the qualitative.
8. Behavioral objectives are appropriate for typing or machine shop, but not for history or literature.
9. The concept of behavioral objectives and performance is sometimes misinterpreted as implying that no outcomes of learning are important except overt behavior.
10. Stating in advance precisely what should happen in a class precludes much significant and valuable incidental learning.
11. Precise objectives tend to preclude readjustments as the learning activities proceed.
12. The writing of behavioral objectives requires far too much time for the good that results.

Summary Assessment

During the late 1960's educators and the public increasingly sensed discrepancies between high-sounding educational goals and student performance. Upon closer examination, the objectives appeared so vague and elusive that educators and critics of schools lacked common ground for assessing the effectiveness of education and for planning what many considered an urgently needed revitalization.

The absence of clear objectives handicapped evaluation of innovative practices, novel school organization, and new materials and equipment. The inability to measure recognizable performance in relation to commonly accepted goals continued to puzzle researchers and taxpayers. Rapid change in values and attitudes raised questions concerning the proper affective role of the school, the responsibility of the home and church, education versus indoctrination, the effectiveness of various approaches to teaching values, and many other perplexing problems. As a result, the need has been clear for objectives stated in precise behavioral terms, for instructional programs designed to achieve the objectives, and for evaluation procedures that provide observable evidence that the desired ends have been attained.

National assessment is under way. Collective negotiations in education are rapidly becoming common practice. PPBS (Planning, Programming, Budgeting System), performance contracting, and the voucher method all propose to relate input to output. Goals must be determined, and results must be measured. Accountability requires clearly stated objectives and valid means of assessing performance.

Behavioral objectives will contribute significantly to all these efforts. They have already accomplished much by giving meaning and validity to many aspects of teaching, learning, and evaluation. Continued study, practice, and research will improve the process and increase the benefits. Progress will continue toward further developing materials and learning activities that are actually related to the attainment of desired outcomes. Meaningless results, neglect of the affective areas of learning, and irrelevant assignments will come under close scrutiny. Effective development of understandable objectives promises to facilitate growth in self-direction both on the part of the teacher and the student. It should be an invaluable aid to independent study for out-of-school adults as well as for children by enabling them to set their goals, focus their learning, and assess their progress.

A Few Leaders in the Movement

Robert Armstrong	H. M. Harmes	Robert Mager
Benjamin S. Bloom	Robert Kibler	B. B. Mosia
Lee Cronbach	D. R. Krathwohl	Ralph Ojemann
John B. Gilpin	H. H. McAshan	W. I. Popham

A Few Places Where the Innovation Is Used

Bloomfield Hills, Mich.	Hillsborough County, Fla.	Sioux Falls, S.D.
Carlisle, Pa.	Mt. Healthy, Ohio	University of Ill.
Carson City, Nev.	Norwalk, Conn.	University of Neb.
Edina, Minn.	Portland, Oreg.	Westerly, R.I.

Bibliography

Armstrong, Robert, Terry Cornell, Robert Kraner, and E. Wayne Roberson, *The Development and Evaluation of Behavioral Objectives.* Worthington, Ohio: Charles A. Jones, 1970.

Atkin, J. Myron, "Behavioral Objectives in Curriculum Design: A Cautionary Note," *The Science Teacher*, XXXV, No. 5 (1968), 27-30.

Bloom, Benjamin S., ed., *Taxonomy of Educational Objectives, The Classification of Educational Goals, Handbook I: Cognitive Domain.* New York: McKay, 1956.

Caffyn, Lois, "Behavioral Objectives: English Style," *Elementary English*, XLV, No. 8 (1968), 1073-1074.

Cronbach, Lee J., *Educational Psychology.* New York: Harcourt, 1963.

Haberman, Martin W., "Behavioral Objectives: Breakthrough or Bandwagon," in *Reading in Curriculum*, eds. Glen Hass, Kimball Wiles, and Joseph Bondi, pp. 394-397. Boston: Allyn and Bacon, 1970.

Harmes, H.M., *Behavioral Analysis of Learning Objectives.* West Palm Beach, Fla.: Harmes, 1969.

Kibler, Robert J., Larry L. Barker, and David T. Miles, *Behavioral Objectives and Instruction.* Boston: Allyn and Bacon, 1970.

Krathwohl, David R., Benjamin S. Bloom, and Bertram B. Masia, *Taxonomy of Educational Objectives, The Classification of Educational Goals, Handbook II: Affective Domain.* New York: McKay, 1964.

McAshan, H.H., *Writing Behavioral Objectives.* New York: Harper, 1970.

Mager, Robert F., *Preparing Instructional Objectives.* Palo Alto, Calif.: Fearon, 1962.

Montague, Earl J. and David P. Butts, "Behavioral Objectives," *The Science Teacher*, XXXV, No. 3 (1968), 33-35.

Ojemann, Ralph H., "Should Educational Objectives Be Stated in Behavioral Terms?" *Elementary School Journal*, LXIX, No. 5 (1969), 229-235.

Popham, W.I. and E.L. Baker, "Measuring Teachers' Attitudes Toward Behavioral Objectives," *Journal of Educational Research*, LX, No. 10 (1967), 453-455.

Simpson, Elizabeth Jane, *Taxonomy of Educational Objectives, The Classification of Educational Goals, Handbook III, Psychomotor Domain.* Worthington, Ohio: Charles A. Jones, forthcoming.

Performance Contracting 9

Definition

Performance contracting is a procedure by which a school system enters into a contract with a business to carry out a specific instructional task such as teaching reading or mathematics. For a stipulated amount of money, the firm guarantees to produce specific results within a specified period of time.

Many of the problems which schools face today are the inevitable result of inability to keep abreast of change. Throughout the years, very few school budgets have included a single dollar specifically allocated to research and development. Taxpayers have resisted higher taxes, and teachers organizations have demanded the lion's share of additional funds. In the meantime, private industry has sensed a vast market for educational programs. The federal government has encouraged private research agencies to explore new approaches to solving knotty social and educational problems. They have examined the possibility of applying new technology to some of these problems and of assuring accountability for their solution.

During recent years research bureaus and educational development centers have sprung up throughout the country. The widely publicized contract of the Texarkana schools with a private firm is an example of guaranteed performance. The objective was to reduce dropouts by improving reading and mathematic skills of retarded students.

In 1970 the Office of Economic Opportunity launched an experiment involving approximately 28,000 students to test efficacy of performance contracting. The study was designed to test the effect of technological aids, incentives, and other instructional devices on learning mathematics and reading skills. The focus is on children in grades 1-3 and 7-9 selected from low-income families who lack motivation and interest because of repeated failure in competition with their peers. The United States Office of Education has funded six similar programs.

Contracts between the schools and business firms are for the attainment of specific objectives. Most frequently they are limited to reading and mathematics, but other areas such as vocational information are beginning to appear. Instruction is characterized by extensive use of rewards, pleasant surroundings, teaching machines, multi-media aids, reorganized tests, teacher aides, small classes, and individualized instruction.

Significant Components — *Which are essential?*

1. Care must be exercised to distinguish between education and miseducation.
2. Public and private enterprise must weld a solid partnership in order to avoid destructive competition and conflict between the schools and industry.
3. Understanding and support from professional organizations of teachers must be developed.
4. Improved learning, rather than financial savings, must be the basic consideration.
5. Results of performance contracting must be assessed by an independent agency.
6. Safeguards must be established to prevent teaching only those areas included in the contract to the neglect of other important outcomes.
7. The permanence of learning and its transferability to solving related problems must be given special consideration.
8. To assure maximum benefit for inservice development, local teachers and administrators must be deeply involved.
9. The objectives must be clear and specific, the instruction sound and relevant.
10. Advertising and exploitation on the part of the contractor must be prevented.
11. The contracting firm's capability to perform is essential.
12. The evaluation should test for process as well as for knowledge and skill.

13. Assessment must be specific enough to evaluate the attainment of the contracted objectives, yet broad enough to avoid overemphasis on minutiae.
14. Competitive bidding among firms is important.
15. The improvement of staff through the demonstration of new aids to teaching and learning must be recognized as a valuable outcome and pursued systematically.

Proposed Advantages *With which ones do you agree?*

1. Performance contracting stimulates experimentation and discovers valuable new ways of promoting learning.
2. Contracting is based on the sound principle of accountability and develops a procedure for applying it to teaching.
3. Efficiency provides better education for the same money.
4. Performance contracting avoids fuzzy thinking by insisting on precise, clearly-stated, and significant objectives whose achievement can be identified and measured.
5. Unlike education, industry understands the value of research, and industrial budgets demonstrate commitment to searching for better methods and products.
6. Industry approaches challenges with a positive attitude which assumes that no problem is too difficult or too costly to solve, while schools constantly complain that they could do many things better if they had the money.
7. Since private enterprise is close to the realities of life, its ideas project an educational program more relevant to the needs of society.
8. Performance contracting proposes to supplement, not replace, conventional programs and to assist schools in installing new programs.
9. Opportunity for further refinement and expansion into the affective areas of learning is limited only to the extent of the imagination of educational and industrial leaders, their determination to meet the challenge, and their willingness to work together.
10. Because accountability and performance contracting have been well received by the general public, they increase community support for schools.
11. Industry has had long and successful experience with analyzing all factors of input as they contribute to output.
12. The profit incentive places at the disposal of education the vast capabilities of corporations.
13. Competition stimulates interest, increases effort, and demands continuous search for better ways of achieving goals.

14. Accountability forces schools to give higher priority to achieving results than to custodial care of children.
15. For the first time boards of education have a basis from which to discharge their responsibility for evaluating the effectiveness of their programs.

Criticisms and Difficulties to Be Anticipated

Do you agree?

1. Performance contracting moves control of education away from the local community to national corporations and the federal government.
2. Performance contracting is geared to machines and mechanistic learning.
3. Performance contracting sounds the knell of public education as we have known it in America.
4. There is a danger of prostituting teaching to achieve immediately observable results.
5. A democratic society cannot afford to promote an educational program that sows the seeds for its own destruction by neglecting societal needs.
6. A real danger exists of developing a generation of programmed people.
7. Mutual understanding, commonality of experience, respect of man for man, and cohesiveness are given only casual attention.
8. Results of performance contracting cannot be compared with those of the conventional classroom because they are secured in small classes with an abundance of expensive equipment.
9. It is difficult to compare the activities of performance contracting with those of the regular school program.
10. Profit-making firms will exploit education; nobody should be allowed to profit from the education of children.
11. Performance contractors oversimplify the purpose and problems of education and overemphasize minutiae and highly organized routines for developing skills.
12. Many of the conflicts between citizens, students, and schools have sprung from the impersonal nature of our urban-industrial society. Now the agencies that helped to create the problem propose to solve it by greater depersonalization.
13. Performance contracting is excessively expensive.
14. Teaching to the test can be controlled, but teaching to the narrow specifications of the contract will become established practice.
15. Great teachers regularly devote much time to guiding and inspiring students in invaluable ways that will never be reflected in test results.

16. The pressure of accountability as conceived in performance contracting will force great teachers to become drill masters, dispensers of information, and developers of fads and mechanistic skills.

Summary Assessment

The proponents of turning more of education over to private enterprise stress the point that public education is in dire trouble because of its failure to experiment with new approaches to meeting the needs of disadvantaged youth, lack of incentives for students and teachers, and resistance to technological advances. They believe private enterprise will bring the stimulation of competition, new perspective, and vast human and material resources to a floundering educational system that has lost public confidence. Some educators point out that industry too is in dire trouble. Young people express serious dissatisfaction with the schools; but these same youngsters are perhaps more deeply disturbed about what they conceive of as selfish and materialistic interests of private enterprise. They blame industry for contributing to making war possible, for polluting the environment, for exploiting minority groups, and for disregarding the interests of the consumer.

A large-city superintendent, confused by performance contracting, raises a few challenging questions. "Where have all these experts been all these years," he asks, "while the board, staff, and citizens in our city have been searching for better ways of coping with our perplexing problems? Why didn't they come forth with some of their simple answers to help us before things got to the point of bankruptcy? Now that I am ready to retire, they say they have gadgets and tricks that will guarantee results or your money back. What about all our blood, sweat, and tears?"

The new manager of learning replies, "The trouble with your superintendent is that he retired at the dawn of the electronic age, and the public forgot to take him off the payroll. We were ready to help him, but he and his teachers were always suspicious and defensive. They thought experience was the mother of invention, and that we had gimmicks to sell."

Perhaps the proponents and opponents of performance contracting do not have the same idea of what a good education is, or what accountability means. Perhaps some of them do not want to understand one another. Educators and industrial leaders must, at this point, join hands to prevent the education of children from becoming a football in a competitive struggle. Unless they do, there's a stormy road ahead for performance contracting.

A Few Leaders in the Movement

Charles L. Blaschke	Lloyd Homme	Ronald Schwartz
Lloyd Dorsett	Howard Johnson	Billy B. Sharp
Stanley Elam	Leon Lessinger	George Stern

A Few Places Where the Innovation Is Used

Dallas, Tex.	Gary, Ind.	San Diego, Calif.
Dayton, Ohio	Philadelphia, Pa.	San Francisco, Calif.
Detroit, Mich.	Portland, Oreg.	Texarkana, Ark.
Duluth, Minn.	Providence, R.I.	State of Virginia

Bibliography

Beaven, Keith, "Rewarded With Transistors, Sweaters, Stamps and Stock," *The Times Educational Supplement*, No. 2857 (1970), 16.

Blaschke, Charles, Peter Briggs, and Reed Martin, "The Performance Contract — Turnkey Approach to Urban School System Reform," *Educational Technology*, X, No. 9 (1970), 45-48.

Carlson, Elliot, "Education and Industry: Troubled Partnership," *Saturday Review*, LIII, No. 33 (1970), 45-47, 58-60.

Cass, James, "Profit and Loss in Education," *Saturday Review*, LIII, No. 33 (1970), 39-40.

Donovan, Hedley, ed., "Free Enterprise for Schools," *Time*, XCVIII, No. 8 (1970), 58, 60.

Elam, Stanley, "The Age of Accountability Dawns in Texarkana," *Phi Delta Kappan*, LI, No. 10 (1970), 509, 511-514.

———, "Where the Action is in Performance Contracting," *Phi Delta Kappan*, LI, No. 10 (1970), 510.

Elliott, Lloyd H., "Education at a Profit?" *Educational Record*, LI, No. 1 (1970), 53-56.

Filogamo, Martin J., "Texarkana Battles 'Dropout Dilemma'," *Elementary English*, XLVII, No. 2 (1970), 305-308.

Gillis, James C., Jr., "Performance Contracting for Public Schools," *Educational Technology*, XI, No. 5 (1969), 17-20.

Hickman, L.C., ed., "How Education Groups View Contracting," *Nation's Schools*, LXXXVI, No. 4 (1970), 86-87.

Lessinger, Leon M., "Four Key Ideas to Strengthen Public Education," *Journal of Secondary Education*, XLV, No. 4 (1970), 147-151.

Lipsitz, Lawrence, ed., "Performance Contracting as Catalyst for Reform," *Educational Technology*, IX, No. 8 (1969), 5-9.

Schwartz, Ronald, "Performance Contracting," *Nation's Schools*, LXXXVI, No. 3 (1970), 53-55.

National Assessment 10

Definition

National assessment is a nationwide program for evaluating the outcomes of education by means of written tests, interviews, observation of performance, and other techniques. Its purpose is to find out what large groups of students have and have not learned so that intelligent decision-making regarding improvement of education may be based on reliable information.

The sample is made up of four cross-sectional age groups: nine-year-olds representing those who have completed primary instruction, thirteen-year-olds who have finished elementary school, seventeen-year-olds at the end of their secondary programs, and adults between the ages of twenty-six and thirty-five. Ten areas of learning are being studied: (1) science, (2) writing, (3) citizenship, (4) literature, (5) mathematics, (6) social studies, (7) music, (8) reading, (9) art, and (10) occupational knowledge.

The findings are being reported for the northeastern, southeastern, central, and western regions of the country. The four types of sample communities are large city, urban fringe, small city, and rural town. Socioeconomic status is divided into two groups — those above and those below the poverty level. Provision is made for distinguishing between the performance of boys and girls.

Three or four subject areas are studied each calendar year following a cycle which comes back to each subject every three to five years. Sciences, writing, and citizenship were selected for the year 1969, when the program began by assessing the progress of seventeen-year-olds in March of that year. The evaluation turned to adults during the summer and to elementary pupils during the autumn. Funds for the initial effort were supplied by the Carnegie Corporation, the Ford Foundation, and the United States Office of Education. The annual cost of the assessment is estimated at about five million dollars.

The program is not one of individual testing. Each student takes only one-twelfth of the total test items, and a score is not derived for any individual. Group results are not being compiled for states or school districts. The program plan, objectives, and assessment procedures were developed by the Exploratory Committee on Assessing the Progress of Education established in 1964. In 1969 the Education Commission of the States assumed responsibility for managing the project.

Significant Components *Which are essential?*

1. The promised and established procedure of assessing large groups, rather than individual students or schools, must be zealously guarded lest the bitter battle of the middle 60's between the proponents and opponents of national assessment be renewed with even greater intensity.
2. The program must continue to be controlled by a responsible agency.
3. Long-term, stable financial support is necessary.
4. Provision must be made for modifying objectives and assessment procedures to keep abreast of rapid societal changes.
5. The program must be free from political interference and governmental dictation.
6. Continuous attention must be given to improving the validity of the objectives and to broadening the scope of the assessment to include additional subject fields, out-of-class learning experiences, the affective areas of learning, and learning processes.
7. Objectives and evaluations should include only matters that are worth learning.
8. Teachers, lay citizens, subject area specialists, and those skilled in test construction and other evaluation procedures must work together in establishing objectives and planning the assessment.
9. The national assessment program should refrain from setting standards or drawing implications from the reported findings.
10. Excessive emphasis on cognitive skills, isolated facts, and rote learning must be avoided.

11. The national effort should be coordinated with a total program that will encourage local districts to establish local norms and assess their own programs critically.
12. To be of value, the information secured must be analyzed and followed up with improvement programs in local districts.

Proposed Advantages *With which ones do you agree?*

1. National assessment supplies significant information for making decisions for improving content and processes.
2. Teachers are provided guidelines in establishing objectives, developing strategies, and assessing outcomes.
3. The public has a basis for deciding whether or not it is getting its money's worth.
4. Legislatures and school boards can use the information to establish direction and priorities and for basing actions on facts rather than on personal bias, political pressures, and mass protest.
5. The program provides information relating to differences among various regions, socioeconomic groups, types of communities, sex, and age groups.
6. The program supplies data to defend the schools against irresponsible attacks.
7. A basis for developing a commonality of experiences needed in a highly mobile society is a result of the program.
8. A national effort brings together financial support and personnel that can demonstrate to local districts effective procedures and instruments for assessment.
9. Reporting the per cent of a group that can perform a given task provides data that can be readily understood and interpreted by educators and laymen and used by teachers in their daily work.
10. Traditional programs of evaluation provide information on how well individuals or groups have learned. National assessment reveals what they have or have not learned.
11. National assessment provides information for comparing progress in education over a period of years.
12. The program is a boon to research in every area of teaching and learning.
13. Reliable information for determining which programs should be eliminated, and which ones need to be strengthened is made available.
14. The program provides motivation and resources for developing a broad range of assessment techniques other than paper-and-pencil tests.

Criticisms and Difficulties to Be Anticipated *Do you agree?*

1. National assessment is the first big step that the federal government is taking to assume control of the school curriculum. It is only a small step from national assessment to national testing and another small step to a national curriculum.
2. Federal control will destroy local interest, initiative, and support and remove from local communities and local schools the privilege of deciding what they want their children to learn.
3. Because attitudes and values are difficult to measure, they will be omitted from the assessment and, as a result, neglected by the schools.
4. Those subjects included in the assessment will be stressed to the neglect of other subjects, and teachers will teach for the assessment techniques and instruments.
5. National assessment does not supply information for making decisions for local schools; it makes the decisions.
6. Despite good intentions at present, the program will move toward making comparsions among individuals and districts.
7. Many valuable outcomes of education cannot be measured until the student is out of school for many years.
8. The program provides no help for diagnosing learning deficiencies.
9. Misunderstanding, division, and conflict among parents, teachers, administrators, legislatures, and boards of education develop.
10. Eventually national assessment will establish monolithic standards that disregard unique community needs and inhibit experimentation and search for better approaches to learning.
11. Laymen and administrators are likely to consider success on the items of a national assessment test a complete measure of effective teaching and learning.
12. Since many outside influences that cannot be controlled by the school are included in the assessment, schools will be blamed for all deficiencies of youth.
13. The program is diametrically opposed to individualization of learning.
14. Publishers of textbooks and other materials will focus upon the narrow concepts of the national assessment program.

Summary Assessment

National assessment must be ranked with integration and busing, religion in the classroom, aid to parochial schools, professional negotiations, and teacher strikes as stormy educational issues of recent years. Today the climate is quite different from that of the middle and late 60's. For this the Exploratory Committee on Assessing the Progress of Education deserves great credit. It was the patience, caution, and wisdom with which the committee proceeded in a persistent forward movement that cooled tempers and allayed suspicions. In 1969 the selection of the Education Commission of the States to manage the program also did much to establish confidence and advance the cause. But a degree of mistrust, suspicion, and fear still continues in some quarters.

In the light of the strong opposition to the program during the years of its planning and development, the cooperation of local schools since the actual assessment has gotten under way is surprising and indeed gratifying to those who want to see it succeed. The observation that national assessment establishes the machinery for a more inviting climate for moving toward national testing, national curriculum, and national control cannot be ignored. However, those who have managed since 1964 to avoid making vicious comparisons between schools and between classrooms realize the dangers ahead. Any movement in the direction of making comparisons among schools would surely revive the conflict..

Under good leadership the program may well enhance understanding and cooperation between a restless public and defensive educators. There are few who think that national assessment will cure many of our educational ills, but there are many who believe that it will be a valuable tool to help education chart a better course through its maze of perplexing problems.

A Few Leaders in the Movement

George Brain	Jack Merwin	Ralph Tyler
James Hazlett	John Tukey	Frank Womer

A Few Places Where the Innovation Is Used

Information about national assessment may be secured from Wendell Pierce, Education Commission of the States, 1860 Lincoln Street, Denver, Colorado.

Bibliography

Brain, George B., "What's the Score On National Assessment?" *Today's Education*, LVIII, No. 7 (1969), 18-21.

Donovan, Hedley, ed., "Report Card for Americans," *Time*, XCVI, No. 3 (1970), 38.

Elam, Stanley M., ed., "The Assessment Debate at the White House Conference," *Phi Delta Kappan*, XLVII, No. 1 (1965), 17-18.

———, "Who Should Do the Assessing?," *Phi Delta Kappan*, XLVIII, No. 8 (1967), 377.

Finley, Carmen J., "National Assessment—Spring 1968," *California Journal of Educational Research*, XX, No. 2 (1969), 69-74.

Hand, Harold C., "National Assessment Viewed as the Camel's Nose," *Phi Delta Kappan*, XLVII, No. 1 (1965), 8-13.

Higgins, Martin J. and Jack C. Merwin, "Assessing the Progress of Education," *Phi Delta Kappan*, XLVIII, No. 8 (1967), 378-380.

Kock, Reino, "National Assessment of Education Progress—A Diffusion Study," *School and Society*, XCVII, No. 2315 (1969), 95-97.

Lansner, Kermit, ed., "The National Educational Assessment," *Newsweek*, LXXVI, No. 3 (1970), 40.

McMorris, Robert F., "National Assessment: Coming in 1968-69?," *Phi Delta Kappan*, XLIX, No. 10 (1968), 599-600.

Mehrens, William A., "National Assessment Through September, 1969," *Phi Delta Kappan*, LI, No. 4 (1969), 215-217.

Mollenberg, Wayne P., "National Assessment: Are We Ready?" *The Clearing House*, XLIII, No. 8 (1969), 451-454.

Prakken, Lawrence W., "The National Assessment: Initial Report, Reactions, and Benefits," *The Education Digest*, XXXVI, No. 1 (1970), 1-5.

Shafer, Robert E., "What Can We Expect from a National Assessment in Reading?" *Journal of Reading*, XIII, No. 1 (1969), 3-8.

Turney, David and Burton E. Altman, "National Assessment—Why All the Fuss?" *Educational Leadership*, XXIII, No. 6 (1966), 442-446.

Tyler, Ralph W., "Assessing the Progress of Education," *Phi Delta Kappan*, XLVII, No. 1 (1965), 13-16.

———, "Let's Clear the Air on Assessing Education," *Nation's Schools*, LXXVII, No. 2 (1966), 68-70.

———, "National Assessment—Some Valuable By-Products For Schools," *National Elementary Principal*, XLVIII, No. 6 (1969), 42-48.

Wilson, Thomas E., "In Rebuttal," *Ohio Schools*, XLIV, No. 2 (1966), 15.

Voucher System 11

Definition

The voucher system is a plan for financing elementary and secondary education through the use of certificates which the government gives to parents who have children of school age. The parent selects a school of his choice and presents the certificate as payment for the instruction of the child. The school presents the voucher to the government and receives a check for its services. If a family has several school-age children, it receives a voucher for each child, which can be used at a public school, parochial or private school, or at one operated by a corporation. The value of the voucher and the payment by the government is in the amount established by a formula. The basic value might be the average expenditure per child in a given district or area. Some proposals suggest additional amounts for disadvantaged children going as high as double the basic value of the voucher.

In the spring, parents would indicate to the voucher agency which school each child wants to attend in the autumn. If the particular school is filled, a lottery system might be employed to prevent discrimination. Different plans include provisions for parents to supplement the amount of the voucher, adjusting the value of the certificate upward for disadvantaged children, charging parents additional money for schools that set higher tuition rates, prohibiting schools from accepting supplementary funds, and other arrangements.

The goal of the plan is to improve educational programs by making schools more responsive to the needs of children and the desires of parents. It is hoped that the necessity of choosing an appropriate school for each child will generate a feeling of parental involvement in educational decision-making and of having some control over their children's schooling. This should increase parents' concern about the quality and quantity of their children's education and add to their sense of parental responsibility.

Significant Components — *Which are essential?*

1. Time, patience, experimentation, and careful testing are necessary to allay suspicions and fears of the system.
2. Some kind of regulatory agency will have to be developed for establishing and maintaining standards of quality.
3. The needs of disadvantaged children must be provided for without destroying maximum opportunities for the advantaged.
4. Using vouchers to promote segregation and provincialism should be prevented.
5. The agency administering the voucher system should be an arm of government.
6. It is important that all information about the various schools be made available to the public, including detailed financial reports.
7. Provision should be made for helping parents become more competent in making decisions about the education of their children.
8. Incentive for upgrading programs should be safeguarded.
9. Equal opportunity for all children should be assured regardless of their social, economic, or intellectual status.
10. Misleading claims and fraud must be dealt with promptly and decisively.
11. Parents should be assisted in assuming increased responsibility.
12. Cooperation and support of boards of education, administrators, and teachers are essential.

Proposed Advantages — *With which ones do you agree?*

1. The voucher system would make schools more responsive to the needs of children and the desires of parents.

2. It would encourage parents to assume greater responsibility for planning the education of their children and make them more supportive of education.
3. The plan would provide the same freedom of choice for the poor that is now open only to the wealthy.
4. The poor would have a part in educational planning, improvement, and decision-making.
5. The plan would tend to break up large, cumbersome, and ineffective schools.
6. The voucher system follows the principle of consumer sovereignty and would improve existing public and private schools by the addition of economic incentive.
7. The plan provides incentives that would make children who are hard to educate welcome applicants for admission.
8. Compensatory models follow the principle, long observed in hospitals, of devoting greater resources and providing the best services to those who need them most.
9. If, because of excessive personal conflict, a child developed an emotional block against one school, he could transfer to another.
10. Administrators and teachers would be urged to consider innovative strategies and to experiment with improved approaches to teaching and learning.
11. Good schools would become better because of increased moral and financial support, and poor schools would improve or go out of business.
12. Eventually schools would make better provision for all children, but particularly for the talented and the disadvantaged. The common tendency of teachers to teach to the middle of the population would be reduced.
13. Competition would shake present complacency of the public schools and stimulate more concern and greater effort.
14. The voucher system would be a welcome aid to thousands of deserving parochial schools.
15. Parents who seek highly academic programs or those who want to emphasize moral and spiritual values could find schools to meet their desires.

Criticisms and Difficulties to Be Anticipated

Do you agree?

1. Parents would be confused and frustrated because they would be required to exercise more responsibility than they are capable of or willing to accept.

2. The system is an invitation for hucksters to make money by deceiving parents, particularly parents of disadvantaged children.
3. The government would be called upon for massive funding of plant and equipment for fly-by-night speculators who might leave the building within a short time.
4. Instability of future enrollment and support would make long-term planning impossible for the public schools.
5. The public schools would gradually become the dumping ground for children rejected by other schools.
6. Problems of transportation would be multiplied as children shuttle back and forth, to and from the schools of their choice. The system would be like running power lines for a dozen companies operating in the same community.
7. Duplication of expensive buildings and equipment would be tremendously wasteful.
8. The advances made through school consolidation would be wiped out.
9. The idea of free choice in selecting schools is built on the premise that educators do not know any more about educating children than the man on the street.
10. Although the public school has always been the poor man's school, advocates of the voucher plan want to replace it with private schools.
11. Competing schools would stress personal gain for the individual and neglect the welfare of society.
12. The voucher system would result in segregation along many lines—racial, social, intellectual, political, economic.
13. The proponents advocate a free, competitive market with strict controls to prevent segregation.
14. Prohibiting parents from supplementing the value of the voucher would be tantamount to making it illegal to provide for developing talented youth to the maximum.
15. Because of its strict regulations to enforce freedom of choice, the plan will create undreamed of conflict.
16. The plan is being promoted by people who are bitter because of some unfortunate experience with the public schools.
17. An unregulated voucher system would discriminate unmercifully against disadvantaged children.
18. Very small schools taught in recreation rooms in the teacher's home would spring up everywhere.
19. Under an unregulated plan, affluent citizens would vote against public support and provide the quality of education that they desire by supplementing the worth of the vouchers; and public schools would deteriorate rapidly.

20. Variations in the value of vouchers would result in continual personal strife and legal conflict.
21. Sensationalism, gadgets, and gimmicks are likely to be used to attract and retain students.
22. Children would move to a different school whenever their teachers tried to discipline them.
23. Elaborate and costly machinery will have to be established to combat abuses and fraud.
24. The chief argument against the system, proposed by well-meaning theorists, is that it simply will not work.

Summary Assessment

The educational voucher system faces a long, hard struggle. Many people are deeply concerned about inequality in our public schools, particularly the lack of opportunity for disadvantaged and poor children. They sense a feeling of indifference or resignation on the part of too many administrators and teachers. Public education, they believe, has become a bankrupt monopolistic bureaucracy. But the opponents of the voucher system are even more passionate in their condemnation of what they conceive of as a sinister and vicious scheme to destroy American education.

Even the most sincere critics of public education may be overlooking the serious concerns and dedicated efforts of hundreds of thousands of competent educators. Nevertheless, some of their feelings of urgent need for changing many aspects of school programs may be well grounded. On the other hand, the thought of splintering the American system of free public education, which has served the nation well, arouses fear and anxiety among many educators and laymen alike. They will resist what they consider a breakdown of the bulwark of educational opportunity to repair some of its defects.

The report of the Office of Economic Opportunity puts the problem this way:

> Indeed, an unregulated voucher system could be the most serious setback for the education of disadvantaged children in the history of the United States. A properly regulated system, on the other hand, could inaugurate a new era of innovation and reform in American schools.*

---

*Christopher Jencks, et al., *Education Vouchers* (Cambridge, Mass.: Center for the Study of Public Policy, 1970), p. 17.

Harold Spears, distinguished educator, replies that if the voucher plan is broadly accepted,

> The hand of tradition in American education would be scorched by the fire of criticism, and new ideas would spring up all over the place. You might even find a completely automated school with personnel limited to repairmen; education as well as food dispensed by machines.*

If the voucher system is to make a positive contribution to American education, it must be nurtured by a thoughtful blending of innovation and tradition, impulse and reflection, action and caution, energy and patience, theory and practice.

---

*Harold Spears, "Please Get in Line for Your Voucher," *The School Administrator*, The American Association of School Administrators, summer 1970, p. 12.

A Few Leaders in the Movement

Christopher Jencks	Theodore Sizer	Phillip Whitten

Places Contemplating Use of Vouchers

Hartford, Conn.	Milwaukee, Wis.	Pittsburgh, Pa.
Kansas City, Mo.	Oakland, Calif.	San Francisco, Calif.

Bibliography

Cohodes, Aaron, "Voucher System Gets Chance to Show How it Would Work," *Nation's Schools*, LXXXVI, No. 3 (1970), 20.

Donovan, Hedley, ed., "Free Enterprise For Schools," *Time*, XCVIII, No. 8 (1970), 58, 60.

Elliott, Osborn, ed., "Pay-As-You-Go-Schooling," *Newsweek*, LXXVI, No. 6 (1970), 49.

Hill, Frederick W., "Voucher System—Ban or Boon?" *Business Management*, XLII, No. 11 (1970), 16-17.

Jencks, Christopher, "Education Vouchers," *The New Republic*, CLXI, No. 1 (1970), 19-21.

Jencks, Christopher, et. al., *Education Vouchers, A Preliminary Report on Financing Education by Payments to Parents*. Cambridge, Mass.: Center for the Study of Public Policy, 1970.

Sizer, Theodore and Philip Whitten, "A Proposal For a Poor Children's Bill of Rights," *Psychology Today*, II, No. 3 (1968), 59-63.

Spears, Harold, "Please Get in Line for Your Voucher," *The School Administrator*, The American Association of School Administrators, summer 1970.

Waters, Harry, ed., "Pay-As-You-Go-Schooling," *Newsweek*, LXXVI, No. 6 (1970), 49.

Part Three
Curriculum Expansion and Improvement

Creativity Development 12

Definition

E. Paul Torrance defines creativity as "the process of sensing problems or gaps in information, forming ideas or hypotheses, testing and modifying these hypotheses, and communicating the results. Creativity has also been defined," he says "as a successful step into the unknown, getting away from the main track, breaking out of the mold, being open to experience and permitting one thing to lead to another, recombining ideas or seeing new relationships among ideas, and so on."* He also accepts defining creativity in terms of an original product.

Many people take the position that testing ideas, revising them, and retesting them is more a process of problem solving than of creativity. They conceive of creativity as being a process that is different, distinct, and unusual. Feasibility and productivity assume significance subordinate to originality of the idea, new perspective, and expansion of personality.

Creativity development involves encouraging the student to be curious, resourceful, and inventive. Most important is his thinking.

---

*E. Paul Torrance, *Creativity* (Washington, D.C.: The National Education Association, 1963), p. 4.

His desires and his efforts are directed toward producing or stimulating something that is uniquely his. He must feel the urge to go beyond learning from others by accepting their ideas, to learning from personal, innovative discovery and invention. This can come about only through building individual confidence. Creativity is self-perpetuating in that new discoveries rekindle curiosity. The old idea that there is only one correct answer is discarded. However, thought must still be given to consideration of what is ethically and morally right.

Significant Components — *Which are essential?*

1. Only the creative teacher can truly develop creativity.
2. An open, relaxed atmosphere is necessary to foster the development of creativity.
3. Children must be encouraged and stimulated to experiment and discover for themselves.
4. Limitations and mistakes should be accepted as normal.
5. Teachers and pupils must feel free to fail in their search for answers; they must realize that even when they "fail," they are likely to have learned something valuable.
6. Students should be rewarded for exploring strange approaches and coming out with unique relationships.
7. Flexible schedules and unstructured periods are helpful for promoting imagination and discovery.
8. Teachers must plan for teaching creativity as they plan for achieving other objectives.
9. Inservice experiences to probe factors that stifle creativity development are worthwhile.
10. A stimulating environment with many varied materials and experiences contributes to the program.
11. Open-endedness enhances the potential for fostering creativity.
12. Rigid conformity and creativity are incompatible.
13. New experiences, new problems, new challenges stimulate growth in creativity.
14. Teachers must believe in the discovery method.
15. Opportunity should be provided for meditation, reflective thought, and even daydreaming.
16. Grades, competition, and comparisons between individuals should be minimized.
17. Questioning and challenging should be encouraged.

Proposed Advantages *With which ones do you agree?*

1. New ideas and approaches to solving problems are likely to occur when the possible answers to a problem are unlimited.
2. Today's society places a high premium on originality and has a great need for it.
3. Imaginative people are more successful than less imaginative ones in school work and later as adults.
4. In this day of machines which store and retrieve information better than people, people are needed who relate data in novel ways.
5. Creative students usually are flexible in shifting their behavior to meet new problems. They can tolerate or respond to events or situations that they do not fully understand, disagree with, or cannot control.
6. Creative students discover new areas of interest and ability and usually pursue them with enthusiasm and vigor.
7. Self-expression contributes to self-realization and self-adjustment.
8. Originality enhances the child's chances of achieving his fullest potentialities because it develops his confidence in his own original ideas.
9. Creative students are sympathetic to the uniqueness of others.
10. Creating something new and different is a source of self-satisfaction.
11. Powers of communication and self-expression are improved.
12. The inner resources of the individual are aroused and strengthened.
13. Most of the significant discoveries of man have sprung from creative impulses.
14. The creative person can better cope with the dehumanizing pressures of conformity in our society.
15. Creativity adds meaning and significance to whatever the child is learning.

Criticisms and Difficulties to Be Anticipated *Do you agree?*

1. Many teachers are uncomfortable and insecure when a free and open climate exists in the classroom.
2. Insistence on creativity destroys conformity.
3. Creativity development is often thought to be limited to certain kinds of subject areas.
4. People tend to distrust what is new, different, and potentially upsetting.

5. An informal classroom may appear to lack planning, organization, and control on the part of the teacher.
6. Unique responses are frequently not "correct" responses.
7. Creativity may appear to disrupt logical and orderly pursuit of learning.
8. Many administrators do not understand the conditions that are conducive to creativity development and therefore misinterpret or resent them.
9. Parents often condemn creative behavior and look upon it as an abnormality.
10. Creativity is sometimes considered inimical to systematic problem solving and maximum achievement.
11. Teachers often do not know that creative thinking can be stimulated nor how to stimulate it.
12. There is a lack of evidence concerning the effects of various instructional approaches.
13. Teachers may expect all bright children to be creative and the less gifted to be incapable of creative thinking and expression.
14. Creative pupils are frequently scorned by their classmates.
15. Many students feel repressed and lack the courage to launch out into the unknown and face the possibility of failure.
16. It is often difficult to distinguish between creative thinking and careless thinking.
17. Many teachers do not realize that creativity can be defined and has different stages of growth.
18. Unless divergent thinking takes place within a relatively stable setting, it may destroy whatever exists.

Summary Assessment

Dissidence, lack of self-identity, and abandonment of age-old values by youth are frequently ascribed to too much permissiveness on the part of parents and teachers. Quite the opposite could be true. Insistence on conformity may cause extreme frustration in students with high creative potential, driving them to resistance, nonconformity, and even anger. Self-discovery can be achieved through the release of the creative energy of the inner self, but individuality must be balanced with concern for the rights and well-being of others. Equally important is a willingness to accept the degree of conformity necessary to safeguard those rights. Truly creative students are perhaps best equipped to cope with necessary conformity because their minds are busy creating new ideas, acceptable diversions, and adequate adjustments. An integrated personality requires confidence built upon the student's pride in his unique contributions. Spontaneity and initiative depend upon freedom to explore and to express oneself through ideas and behavior that are genuinely his own.

There seems to be consensus that creativity can be developed, and that the schools should address themselves to developing it. Many of the really significant contributions to society have been made by those who think imaginatively and discover new approaches to the solution of perplexing problems. Hence, serious study should be directed toward discovering new and more effective ways of fostering creativity that lends to self-realization without infringing on the well-being of others.

A Few Leaders in the Movement

H. H. Anderson
Paul B. Diederich
Doris Young Kuhn
Donald MacKinnon
George E. Monroe
Walter T. Petty
Otto Rank
Geraldine Siks
James A. Smith
C. E. Spearman
Calvin Taylor
E. Paul Torrance

A Few Places Where the Innovation Is Used

Centerville, Ohio
Dayton, Ohio
Eastern Wash. State Coll.
Lansing, Mich.
University of Conn.
University of Ga.
University of Utah
Warwick, R.I.
Wayne, Neb.

Bibliography

Brown, George J., "Teaching Creativity to Teachers and Others," *The Journal of Teacher Education*, XXI, No. 2 (1970), 210-216.

Frymier, Jack R. and Horace C. Hawn, *Curriculum Improvement for Better Schools*. Worthington, Ohio: Charles A. Jones, 1970.

Goodlad, John I. and M. Frances Klein, *Behind the Classroom Door*. Worthington, Ohio: Charles A. Jones, 1970.

Gowan, John Curtis, George D. Demos, and E. Paul Torrance, *Creativity: Its Educational Implications*. New York: Wiley, 1967.

Inslow, Gail M., *The Emergent In Curriculum*, pp. 69-89. New York: Wiley, 1966.

Kagan, Jerome, ed., *Creativity and Learning*. Boston: Houghton Mifflin, 1967.

Kravetz, Nathan, "The Creative Child in the Un-Creative School," *The Educational Forum*, XXXIV, No. 2 (1970), 219-222.

Lowenfeld, Viktor, *Creative and Mental Growth*. New York: Macmillan, 1959.

MacKinnon, Donald W., "The Courage to Be: Realizing Creative Potential," *Life Skills in School and Society*, ASCD Yearbook, Washington, D.C.: Association for Supervision and Curriculum Development, 1969.

Neperud, Ronald W., "Artists at Work: A Key to Understanding," *Art Education*, XXIII, No. 2 (1970), 33-35.

Piltz, Albert and Robert Sund, *Creative Teaching of Science in the Elementary School*. Boston, Mass.: Allyn and Bacon, 1968.

Siks, Geraldine Brain, *Creative Dramatics: An Art for Children*. New York: Harper, 1958.

Smith, James A., *Creative Teaching of the Language Arts in the Elementary School*. Boston, Mass.: Allyn and Bacon, 1967.

———, *Creative Teaching of Social Studies*. Boston, Mass.: Allyn and Bacon, 1967.

———, *Setting Conditions for Creative Teaching in the Elementary School*. Boston, Mass.: Allyn and Bacon, 1966.

Taylor, Calvin W., ed., *Creativity: Progress and Potential*. New York: McGraw-Hill, 1964.

Thomas, George I. and Joseph Crescimbeni, *Individualizing Instruction in the Elementary School*, pp. 161-184. New York: Random, 1967.

Torrance, E. Paul, *Creativity*. Washington, D.C.: National Education Association of the United States, 1963.

———, *Guiding Creative Talent*. Englewood Cliffs, N.J.: Prentice-Hall, 1962.

———, *Rewarding Creative Behavior*. Englewood Cliffs, N.J.: Prentice-Hall, 1965.

Torrance, E. Paul and R. E. Myers, *Creative Learning and Teaching*. New York: Dodd, Mead, 1970.

Montessori Method 13

Definition

The Montessori method is an approach to educating preschool children, usually between the ages of three and six, through the performance of simple tasks and the utilization of specially prepared materials and equipment. These materials stress sensory-motor learning and provide for pupils working independently. Thus each child progresses at his own rate. The role of the teacher is to diagnose learning difficulties and to provide each individual child with materials appropriate for overcoming his problems. Although the program is rather precise in structure, its application proceeds on an individualized basis.

The frequency with which it is discussed and the unfamiliarity of the term often leaves the impression that the Montessori method is an innovation. In reality, however, it is a revival of a program prepared by Dr. Maria Montessori in Italy at the beginning of the century. Her medical studies convinced her that an educational program needed to be developed to prevent permanent retardation among poor, deaf, and disadvantaged children.

Today the Montessori revival in the United States has two branches: the Association Montessori Internationale, which uses only orthodox methods and materials; and the American Montessori Society, which uses the original Montessori methods and materials, but also incorporates new equipment and activities into the program.

Significant Components *Which are essential?*

1. Tactile and other materials specially designed for the Montessori method are a basic part of the program.
2. Teachers trained in the Montessori method are essential for guiding activities.
3. Essentially the child is freed from a time schedule.
4. Within broad limits, children are permitted to stay with a given task as long as they want to or to turn to another as soon as they want to.
5. The teacher devotes the major portion of her efforts to diagnosing difficulties and providing for their correction.
6. Having the child ask for help is a significant part of the method.
7. Space and facilities are necessary for freedom of movement and performance of a wide variety of physical tasks.
8. Manners and courtesy toward other children are stressed.
9. The school must ignore the graded concept.
10. Many everyday life situations such as dressing, washing, eating, and looking after his surroundings are incorporated in the child's learning experiences.
11. Responsibility is placed upon the learner to take care of his material and equipment and return it to its proper place when he has finished the task.
12. In the main, children work by themselves and do not interfere with the activities of others.

Proposed Advantages *With which ones do you agree?*

1. Children are freed from the constant supervision of adults, which they experience in kindergartens and nursery schools and in middle- and upper-class homes.
2. Pupils are allowed to progress at their own learning rates.
3. Transfer of experiences from the child's school activities to those which he encounters in the home is facilitated.
4. The method stresses the importance of a positive attitude toward physical work.
5. Working on specific, individual tasks develops the capacity for problem-solving.
6. Valuable training in sensory-motor perception is provided.
7. Abundance of material provides for experimentation and for stimulating curiosity and interest.
8. Originally planned for physically and neurologically handicapped children from homes of the poor, the program now provides value for all types of children.

9. Brighter children may pursue their own interests and tasks appropriate to their maturation levels.
10. Taking care of his own equipment and materials fosters in the pupil a sense of responsibility.
11. Meaning and significance are added to the child's experience by substituting directed activities for free play.
12. Allowing pupils to proceed to reading and writing when they are ready enables many to learn to read and write at a very early age.
13. His contact with physical objects and tasks provides the child with a sense of reality.
14. Planned exercises provide for physical development.
15. His success in completing observable tasks supplies him with satisfaction and builds confidence.
16. Real life situations promote social attitudes and behavior.
17. Working on specific tasks without interruption develops persistence and power of concentration.
18. Courtesy and good manners are emphasized.
19. Working alone promotes independence and self-sufficiency.
20. The low pupil-teacher ratio allows for better instruction.

Criticisms and Difficulties to Be Anticipated *Do you agree?*

1. Properly trained teachers are very difficult to find.
2. High tuition rates in most existing schools limit the clientele to types of children for whom the program was not planned and developed.
3. The emphasis on working on one's own task and rejecting interaction with others neglects social adjustment.
4. Children are not brought into close relationship with others except by their own choosing.
5. The materials are unduly expensive.
6. Manipulation of and encounters with objects dominate the child's experiences to the neglect of imaginative ideas.
7. The permissiveness of the schedule is a handicap for children when they enter a more structured school.
8. Music and art are neglected.
9. The whole program promotes self-centeredness.
10. Some Montessori schools are accused of operating primarily for financial gains.
11. The method is not consistent with many verified principles of child development.

Summary Assessment

Today the Montessori method is most popular in upper middle-class families, many of whom consider it a badge of distinction to have their children enrolled in a Montessori school. The research that stimulated increased interest in early childhood education gave rise to Head Start, growth of nursery schools, and the impressive revival of Montessori. Many of the materials have been reproduced in modified form. Proponents of the movement have perhaps exaggerated its successes, and the opponents seem unwilling to give it reasoned consideration. Thus it has become a matter of considerable controversy. Those who are critical of the generally unstructured programs of nursery schools and kindergartens welcome the planned tasks of Montessori.

The limited research on the subject gives some indication that Montessori children address themselves more directly to tasks than other children of the same age. They also seem to be more oriented to concrete objects and daily life tasks. Children from nursery schools and kindergartens appear to be somewhat more creative and to exhibit greater social orientation. The Montessori program seems to contribute to achievement in sensory-motor skills, and success is reported in preparing brain injured children for conventional programs.

With the passage of time, the American Montessori Society is likely to move farther away from the orthodoxy of the European Association Montessori Internationale, and the nursery schools and kindergartens are apt to continue to explore the use of Montessori methods and materials. Despite its popularity among upper middle-class families, the hope exists that the Montessori method will continue to be used with disadvantaged children in America as it has been in Italy and other parts of the world since its beginning.

A Few Leaders in the Movement

Clara Craig
Dorothy Canfield Fisher
Ann George
Lena Gitter
Cleo H. Monson
R.C. Orem
Yvonne Plamback
Nancy McCormick Rambusch
E. M. Standing
Edward Wakin

A Few Places Where the Innovation Is Used

Baltimore, Md.	Detroit, Mich.	Oak Park, Ill.
Blue Springs, Mo.	Germantown, Pa.	Oklahoma City, Okla.
Cincinnati, Ohio	Greenwich, Conn.	Philadelphia, Pa.
Corpus Christi, Tex.	Mt. Vernon, N.Y.	St. Paul, Minn.
Danbury, Conn.	New Rochelle, N.Y.	Santa Monica, Calif.

Bibliography

Ahlfeld, Kathy, "The Montessori Revival: How Far Will it Go?" *The Nation's Schools*, LXXXV, No. 1 (1970), 75-80.

Brock, Linda, "A Montessori School in Missouri," *School and Community*, LVI, No. 4 (1969), 17-19.

Dreyer, Albert and David Riger, "Cognitive Performance in Montessori and Nursery School Children," *Journal of Educational Research*, LXII, No. 9 (1969), 411-416.

Fisher, Dorothy Canfield, *The Montessori Manual for Teachers and Parents*. Cambridge, Mass.: Bentley, 1964.

Gardner, Riley W., "A Psychologist Looks at Montessori," *Elementary School Journal*, LXVII, No. 2 (1966), 72-83.

Gitter, Lena A., *The Montessori Way*. Seattle, Wash.: Special Child Publications, 1970.

———, *A Strategy for Fighting the War on Poverty* (The Montessori Method as Applied to the Brookhaven Project). Washington, D.C.: Fagan, 1965.

Littledale, Harold, ed., "Montessori Method," *Grade Teacher*, LXXXVII, No. 4 (1969), 58-59.

Montessori, Maria, *Dr. Montessori's Own Handbook*. New York: Schocken, 1965.

———, *The Montessori Elementary Material*. Cambridge, Mass.: Bentley, 1964.

———, *The Montessori Method*. New York: Stokes, 1912.

———, *Spontaneous Activity in Education*. Cambridge, Mass.: Bentley, 1964.

Orem, R. C., *Montessori: and the Special Child*. New York: Capricorn, 1970.

Selman, Elsie and Ruth Selman, "Montessori/68," *Instructor*, LXXVII, No. 5 (1968), 20-22.

Smaridge, Norah, *The Light Within*. New York: Hawthorn, 1965.

Standing, E. M., *The Montessori Revolution in Education*. Fresno, Calif.: Sierra, 1962.

Wakin, Edward, "The Return of Montessori," *Saturday Review*, XLVII, No. 47 (1964), 61-63.

Courtesy Battle Creek, Michigan, Public Schools

Outdoor Education 14

Definition

Outdoor education involves using the out of doors with all its vast resources to help the learner better know and understand the world about him and his place in that world. Through direct learning experiences, involving participation, actual use of skills, and enjoyment, the student comes to appreciate natural phenomena, his relationship to them, his behavioral effect on them, and his dependence upon them. Insights and skills in dealing with natural resources and problems involving the out of doors are developed. With an arousal of interest in nature the basis for meaningful academic study is developed.

Emphasis might be placed upon conservation, ecology, and appreciation of beauty; or perhaps on socialization, group action, democratic living, economic insights, or man's interrelationship to man. In addition to developing environmental awareness and social sensitivity, an adequate approach offers almost limitless possibilities for enriching all phases of the school program. As a supplement to the activities of the classroom, outdoor education usually includes study of plant and animal life, conservation, rock and land formations, astronomy, and ecology. It is carried out by means of camping, school farms, hiking, construction of various facilities, garden projects, art activities, and recreational pursuits.

Significant Components *Which are essential?*

1. To be vital, an outdoor education program must be carried on out of doors.
2. The program should have definite purposes and well-defined objectives.
3. The program's purposes and activities should be coordinated with the work of most classrooms; it should not be treated as a separate subject.
4. A balance should be maintained among expansion of knowledge and understanding, development of skills, furtherance of wholesome social relationships, deepening of aesthetic appreciations, and promotion of recreational outlets.
5. Only teachers with imagination and awareness of the multifold learning opportunities in the world beyond the classroom can pursue the program with enthusiasm.
6. Direct experience and personal involvement on the part of pupils should be used whenever possible.
7. Minimal facilities and transportation are prerequisites. Elaborate and expensive buildings and equipment are not essential.
8. Careful preplanning and preparation on the part of students and teachers are fundamental.
9. Observation, discovery, involvement, experimentation, work, and play become the prime bases for learning experiences. Teachers must have basic knowledge of natural phenomena and social interaction.
10. The community, board of education, administration, teachers, and pupils must all understand the program and support it.
11. A significant part of the program is the development of abilities in outdoor living, safety, and leisure-time activities.
12. Teachers of all children and all subjects should understand the potentialities of the out of doors.

Proposed Advantages *With which ones do you agree?*

1. Outdoor education provides an inexpensive laboratory for demonstrating the advantages of real experiences utilizing problems and objects to promote learning.
2. It is an effective approach to the inservice improvement of teachers through involvement with their students in new and different dimensions of teaching and learning.
3. Students are aided in understanding their relationships to their natural environment.

4. Vast resources for outdoor learning are near many school buildings, often on the school grounds.
5. The out of doors offers a real and invaluable laboratory to supplement the work of most classrooms. It provides experiences that effectively demonstrate cause and effect relationships.
6. Physical involvement is provided as a relief from the sedentary pursuits and continuous verbalization of the typical classroom.
7. Many motor skills can be effectively developed in the out of doors.
8. Students develop a close relationship with one another and with their teacher, which carries over into their work in the school.
9. Urban children are provided with a basis for assessing their own environment through comparison with another.
10. Self-reliance, keen observation, careful analysis and synthesis, and application of understandings to the solution of practical problems are reinforced.
11. Outdoor education opens new vistas for leisure-time activities.
12. Firsthand, direct, experiences are more readily retained than those learned through indirect means.
13. The program presents an opportunity to discover new possibilities for careers.
14. An appreciation of nature, a positive attitude toward the conservation of natural resources, and increased knowledge and skill for making a personal contribution toward the improvement of the environment are fostered.
15. The rudiments of economics are best learned in the out of doors.
16. Work and play in the out of doors give unity and completeness to human personality.
17. The study of natural phenomena provides a solid base for sex education and family living.
18. Outdoor education gives enriched meaning to our historical origins and cultural heritage.
19. A basis is provided for understanding and appreciating the values of the American frontier.
20. Humility is promoted through vividly demonstrating man's inability to cope with many phenomena of nature. The student is assisted in establishing his self-identity.
21. Contact with the forces of nature develops a sense of personal responsibility and the realization that blame cannot be shifted to someone else when things do not turn out well.
22. Natural beauty deepens patriotism by developing in the young person appreciation of his country and his legacy.

Criticisms and Difficulties to Be Anticipated *Do you agree?*

1. The cost of adequate facilities, particularly for school camps, may be excessive.
2. Transportation is costly and often difficult to obtain.
3. Children are apt to be exposed to undue physical danger.
4. In many areas, state school legislation poses problems.
5. Children in the inner city, who need outdoor education most, are farthest removed from opportunities for it.
6. Teachers lack the knowledge and skill to perform effectively.
7. Time will be diverted from more important areas of learning.
8. Land and camping facilities are difficult to find and costly to acquire and use if they can be found.
9. Teachers are not prepared, nor being prepared, in this field.
10. Many teachers are reluctant to accept the added responsibility and the additional effort required for an effective program.
11. The community may consider outdoor education a frill, a waste of time and money.
12. Although the benefits that may accrue from the program sound good, the danger exists that the results will not match the hopes.

Summary Assessment

For a number of reasons, perhaps, the growth of programs in outdoor education has been slow. School and community leaders have not comprehended its goals and recognized its possibilities. Similarly, teachers have not quickly seen the potentialities of this direct contact with various aspects of the environment. Many have had an exaggerated impression of the cost of an effective program. Continuous shortage of funds in most school districts has prevented school leaders from making even a modest beginning. Absence of trained and interested personnel, coupled with the reluctance of many teachers to put forth the additional time and energy necessary to plan and implement a workable program, has added to the problem.

Recently, however, recognition of the seriousness of pollution, congestion in the large cities and its related problems, nonmotivated children, increased demand for recreational outlets, and desire for environmental improvement have again brought the possibilities of outdoor education to the attention of those who are looking for solutions for community and school problems.

It would appear that vital and well-planned experiences with nature and its influences hold significant promise for improving both educational programs and the environment. Additionally, many social problems might be relieved through direct contact with the out of doors. Perhaps a dramatic change from the concrete walls and asphalt playgrounds of the schools in our teeming urban centers is imperative to enable millions of children to value and respond to a world unknown to them.

Failure to capitalize on the potentialities of education in the out of doors may overlook a promising approach to assisting young people in establishing their identity and in building their life values. Youth seem eager to turn from present-day social, educational, business, and industrial superficialities to the realities of the natural world.

Certainly the problems of pollution will not be solved without greater appreciation and understanding on the part of the leaders and followers of tomorrow. Only through education relating to their natural environment can people learn to live in satisfaction and dignity.

A Few Leaders in the Movement

Albert Brown	Warren C. Gilfillan	Larry McKown
Orval Conner	Mack H. Gillenwater	Dorothy Lou MacMillan
George W. Donaldson	John W. Gilliland	Jack K. Mawdsley
W. R. Evans	Charles Holtzer	L. B. Sharp
M. A. Gabrielson	Richard Kraus	Julian W. Smith

A Few Places Where the Innovation Is Used

Antioch College	McPherson, Kans.	Oregon, Ill.
Battle Creek, Mich.	Mansfield, Ohio	Pacific Grove, Calif.
Frederick County, Md.	Mich. State Univ.	Seattle, Wash.
Indianapolis, Ind.	New Palz, N.Y.	Toledo, Ohio
Jefferson County, Colo.	Northern Ill. Univ.	University of Ind.

Bibliography

Brehm, Shirley A., *A Teachers Handbook for Study Outside the Classroom.* Columbus, Ohio: Merrill, 1969.

Callison, Charles H., *America's Natural Resources.* New York: Ronald, 1967.

Ewald, William R., Jr., ed., *Environment and Change.* Bloomington, Ind.: Indiana University, 1968.

Finlay, Robert, "Schools Without Doors," *Ohio Schools,* XLIII, No. 6 (1965), 15-19.

Gabrielson, M.A. and C. Holtzer, *The Role of Outdoor Education.* New York: The Center for Applied Research in Education, 1965.

Gilfillan, Warren C. and Robert Burgess, *The Counselors' Handbook for the Outdoor School.* Portland, Oreg.: Multnomah Outdoor Education, 1970.

———, *Students' Handbook for the Outdoor School.* Portland, Oreg.: Multnomah Outdoor Education, 1970.

Herbert, Clarke L., "Outdoors with Title III," *National Elementary Principal,* XLVI, No. 2 (1966), 71-75.

Homan, Paul B., "Rugged Path to Outdoor Education," *American School Board Journal,* CLIV, No. 6 (1967), 10-14.

Hug, John W. and Phyllis J. Wilson, *Curriculum Enrichment Outdoors.* Evanston, Ill.: Harper, 1965.

Isenberg, Robert M., "Education Comes Alive Outdoors," *NEA Journal,* LIV, No. 4 (1967), 34-35.

Kraus, Richard, *Recreation Today.* New York: Meredith, 1966.

Lewis, Charles, "Integrating Outdoor Education into the Curriculum," *Journal of Health, Physical Education, and Recreation,* XL, No. 6 (1969), 63-64.

Marsh, Norman, *Outdoor Education on Your School Grounds.* Sacramento: The Resources Agency, State of California, 1968.

Outdoor School Handbook, unpublished curriculum guide. Milwaukie, Oreg.: Milwaukie School District No. 1, 1969.

Outdoors U. S. A. Washington, D.C.: The United States Government Printing Office, 1967.

Revelle, Roger and Hans H. Landsberg, *America's Changing Environment.* Boston: Houghton Mifflin, 1970.

Schramm, Wilbur, "Classroom Out-of-Doors—Part 2," *National Elementary Principal,* XLVIII, No. 6 (1969), 80-96.

Smith, Julian W., et al., *Outdoor Education.* Englewood Cliffs, N.J.: Prentice-Hall, 1963.

Wagner, Guy, "What Schools Are Doing — Promoting Outdoor Education," *Education,* LXXXVI, No. 4 (1965), 248-252.

Williams, Robert J. and Norman G. Rodgers, "Classroom in the Out-of-Doors," *The Bulletin of the National Association of Secondary School Principals,* LIV, No. 344 (1970), 42-47.

Simulation 15

Definition

Simulation is a teaching procedure which uses a model of a real system to provide a lifelike representation to stimulate and aid learning. The representations of the real world may be physical or symbolic and are designed to introduce realism into the learning environment. Symbolic models are usually verbal or mathematical. The mathematical ones are often used to express qualitative relationships in quantitative terms.

The most common forms of simulation are simulation games, dramatization, sociodrama, role playing, case studies, and computerized models. The crucial components of the real situation are incorporated into the constructed model and are presented as verbal descriptions, diagrams, pictures and other symbolic representations. The real environment is limited and simplified so that it can be more readily manipulated. Time and space are usually compressed, and significant aspects of reality are selected.

Gaming refers to a contest between individuals or groups of individuals operating under definite rules and competing for a victory or reward. The game represents life situations for which the players in the game are learning to develop competencies. As the game progresses, the participants play the role of decision-makers and try to achieve established objectives. The reactions of the adversaries provide immediate feedback and redirect the action of the players.

War games have existed for hundreds of years. Chess is often referred to as the oldest of the war games. During the eighteenth century more realistic and complex war games were designed. Engineering early developed physical scale models for constructing machines, buildings, dams, and other projects. For about 15 years, business and industry have used simulated models, particularly for training workers and executives. Dramatization, role playing, and other reproductions of reality have been used in schools since their beginning; but sophisticated models for education have appeared only during the past decade. Much of the early work has been done in the field of social studies with attention being focused on group interaction.

Significant Components *Which are essential?*

1. In order to produce transferable results, the model must possess fidelity in its representation of reality.
2. Purpose and major focus must be clearly understood.
3. Rules for simulation games must be established.
4. The sophistication of the game usually increases its instructional potential.
5. Game designs must result from rigorous experimentation.
6. Simulation of all types should be evaluated in terms of the established objectives.
7. Learners in games must be free to carry out their own decisions, even when making mistakes, and the feedback of the consequences should be rapid and clear.
8. Opportunity and space must be provided for free, uninhibited movement and for flexibility of grouping.
9. An open climate should be maintained, free from leader domination.
10. The scope of the simulation should be limited to selected critical aspects of actions or processes.
11. Creativity on the part of leaders and students is required.
12. Accurate information and facts are essential.
13. Reasonable assurance for intelligent use can be increased by setting significant goals and by previous testing.
14. Simulation should provide for teaching both the cognitive and the affective areas.
15. In the main, decisions must be sufficiently satisfying and rewarding to provide adequate motivation.

16. Provision must be made for developing generalizations.
17. The situation should be repeatable in its original form so that follow-up can be provided.

Proposed Advantages *With which ones do you agree?*

1. Simulation is appealing, motivates intense effort, and increases learning.
2. Success or failure is rapidly and readily recognizable.
3. Vividness, meaning, and potential for greater retention are added.
4. Simulation has demonstrated its power to generate deep emotional involvement.
5. Learning to act by acting, learning to make decisions by making decisions, and learning to solve problems by solving problems are developed.
6. Simulation is particularly effective with under-motivated children.
7. Simulation allows for manipulation by simplifying the complexity of what it represents, thus providing for control of extraneous factors that exist in the real situation.
8. Simulation can be used for the acquisition of information, improvement of new processes, and identification of alternatives in decision-making.
9. A part of life can be selected and specific experiences relating to that part designed.
10. Games lengthen the attention span and develop persistent application to work.
11. Students with a wide range of ability can benefit from playing the same game.
12. Optional starting and stopping are distinct advantages.
13. Factors can be changed if the process indicates need for doing so, and alternate strategies are emphasized.
14. Pupils learn to cope with unpredictable circumstances.
15. Games provide an immediate opportunity to apply learning to the situation of a problem or the attainment of a goal.
16. Games illustrate vividly the relationship between decision-making and its consequences.
17. The need for constant communication between players teaches social interaction.
18. A background of experience essential for developing concepts and principles is given.
19. Simulation can be an aid to all levels of education, with specific value for the education of teachers and administrators.

20. Games are effective in teaching values and attitudes.
21. Simulation provides for critiques of solutions, successes, mistakes, and decisions made.
22. Simulation prevents alienation by involving learners in the environment and by having them accept the responsibility for controlling it.
23. The cost and time necessary for involvement in the real world are reduced.

Criticisms and Difficulties to Be Anticipated — *Do you agree?*

1. At best, simulation is very artificial and oversimplified.
2. Games place too much emphasis on competition.
3. Models are too rigid and narrow in their applicability.
4. Simulation takes too long to get to the heart of a lesson.
5. Loss of fidelity may prevent transferability.
6. The cost is higher than that of other forms of instruction.
7. The process and its analysis are unreasonably complex.
8. Teachers employing simulation may be looked upon as allowing too much freedom and disorder.
9. There is a dearth of personnel qualified to design, implement, and evaluate programs.
10. Games cannot be readily adapted to the peculiar needs of an individual or a particular class.
11. Simulation is not likely to arrive at generalizations necessary for application to different situations.
12. Games are more appropriate for clinical or laboratory use than for the classroom.
13. Gaming and role playing often become activities for activity's sake and fail to provide for transfer; simulation cannot be a substitute for real, direct experience.
14. Games are available in only a few areas.
15. Students who have minor roles lose interest.
16. A complex model confuses; if it is simple, it bores.
17. Limitations of time, machinery, and proper setting may be handicaps.
18. Because of the absence of dangerous consequences of mistakes, simulation may develop a tendency toward irresponsibility in decision-making.
19. The features represented and the outcomes to be achieved are predetermined by the designer, who builds in his own biases.

Summary Assessment

Paralleling the growth in systems analysis, simulation techniques of all kinds are in a stage of rapid experimentation and utilization. In schools, simulations are becoming alternative methods of instruction to the lecture, discussion group, and case study. Research evidence concerning the effectiveness of various simulation techniques is limited. Thus far there is little claim that informational learning is increased, but some evidence indicates that the learning of processes is enhanced. Students become quickly and deeply involved in simulation, enjoy it, and are stimulated to persistent application to work. Although simulation appears to be well adapted to the teaching of values and attitudes, there are mixed reactions concerning its effectiveness in changing behavior.

As the construction and use of models moves forward, increased attention is being given to what the learner is to achieve through use of the model. Using physical, verbal, and mathematical media, the models are employed in the teaching of information, skills, attitudes, values, and behavioral change. During the ensuing years the use of simulation as an instructional tool is likely to grow rapidly as the computer is used more widely.

Contrary to the opinion of many, effective simulation devices can be prepared by classroom teachers. The program will perhaps expand most rapidly in the colleges and high schools. Simulation shows evidence of being an effective technique for working with under-motivated students, and its extended utilization for that group is imminent. Perhaps simulation of all types will move forward most directly in the fields of social studies and other behavioral sciences, where it has been heralded as a promising tool for developing skills in interpersonal interaction. It is also likely to be used more extensively in the training of prospective teachers and educational administrators and supervisors.

A Few Leaders in the Movement

Clark C. Apt
H. O. Belden
James S. Coleman
Donald Cruickshank
Richard E. Dawson
Harold Guetzkow
B. Y. Kersh
James A. Robinson
Fannie R. Shaftel

A Few Places Where the Innovation Is Used

Baltimore, Md.	Mich. State Univ.	South Bend, Ind.
Fort Lauderdale, Fla.	New York, N.Y.	University of Mich.
Johns Hopkins Univ.	Northwestern Univ.	University of Oreg.
Mass. Institute of Tech.	San Francisco, Calif.	University of Wis.

Bibliography

Anderson, Lee F. and Margaret G. Hermann, *A Comparison of Simulation, Case Studies and Problem Papers in Teaching Decision-Making*. Research Project, Northwestern University, 1964.

Boocock, Sarane S. and E.O. Schild, eds., *Simulation Games in Learning*. Beverly Hills, Calif.: Sage, 1968.

Carlson, Elliott, *Learning Through Games*. Washington, D.C.: Public Affairs Press, 1969.

Coleman, James S., "Academic Games and Learning," *National Association of Secondary School Principals Bulletin*, LII, No. 325 (1968), 62-67.

Cruickshank, Donald R., "The Use of Simulation in Teacher Education: A Developing Phenomenon," *The Journal of Teacher Education*, XX, No. 1 (1969), 23-26.

Guetzkow, Harold, ed., *Simulation in Social Science: Readings*. Englewood Cliffs, N.J.: Prentice-Hall, 1962.

Guetzkow, Harold, et al., *Simulation in Interval Relations*. Englewood Cliffs, N.J.: Prentice-Hall, 1963.

Hirsch, Werner Z., et al., *Inventing Education for the Future*. San Francisco: Chandler, 1967.

Hyman, Ronald T., *Ways of Teaching*, pp. 186-198. Philadelphia: Lippincott, 1970.

Raser, John, *Simulation and Society*. Boston: Allyn and Bacon, 1969.

Rogers, Virginia M., "Simulation in Preparing Social Studies Teachers," *Social Education*, XXXIV, No. 3 (1970), 337-340.

Sachs, Stephen M., "The Uses and Limits of Simulation Models in Teaching Social Science and History," *The Social Studies*, LXI, No. 4 (1970), 163-167.

Shaftel, Fannie R., "Role Playing: An Approach to Meaningful Social Learning," *Social Education*, XXXIV, No. 5 (1970), 556-559.

———, *Role-Playing for Social Values: Decision-Making in the Social Studies*. Englewood Cliffs, N.J.: Prentice-Hall, 1967.

Tansey, P. J. and Derick Unwin, *Simulation and Gaming in Education*. London: Methuen, 1969.

Twelker, Paul A., "Designing Simulation Systems," *Educational Technology*, IX, No. 10 (1969), 64-70.

Community Resources 16

Definition

Community resources are precisely what the term implies — the opportunities in the community that can be used to expand and enrich learning experiences for children. These resources may be natural, human, material, or institutional. A wooded canyon, a soldier just returned from Viet Nam, an industrial plant, a family relations court all are rich in their potential for helping teachers and pupils. Social studies, art, science, industrial arts, foreign languages, business education, and essentially all areas of learning can discover rich resources that lie ready to be tapped.

Among the most common approaches are surveys and studies of community problems, interviews, resource persons, study trips, displays of products, audio-visual and printed materials, and service projects. Activities involved in a study trip may range from studying the habits of a beaver family to observing the operation of a blast furnace. Visits may be made to a farmyard or to a cathedral. Equally significant as a resource for teaching and learning are the less tangible resources present in all communities, large or small. They include individual or group relations; historical or cultural development of the community; and business, social, economic, or political problems and processes.

Too frequently human resources within the community have been overlooked. Often volunteers with many varied interests and competencies are able to provide valuable services to schools. Much talent is untapped among retired teachers, legislators, labor leaders, scientists, and other professional men and women. Retired business and industrial leaders, government officials, college professors, farmers, journalists, and zookeepers often enjoy sharing their knowledge and experience with youth. Many high schools have instituted a wide range of community services and study projects. Thousands of secondary students are going far beyond the immediate community to participate in foreign exchange programs during the school year. Many more are traveling and studying abroad during the summer.

The National Community Workshop Association sponsors summer workshops for teachers with academic credit awarded by cooperating universities. The workshops give participants an opportunity to study area resources, visit establishments in the community, and prepare curriculum materials. The oldest of the workshops has operated continuously for two decades.

Significant Components *Which are essential?*

1. Study trips or bringing resource persons to the school requires careful planning.
2. Only knowledgeable resource people who speak effectively and relate well to young people can be of great value.
3. To be justified, study trips should give information or provide motivation not otherwise obtainable.
4. Students should understand clearly what the purpose of the trip is and hence to know what to look for.
5. Those being visited and resource people invited to the school should both know what the purpose is.
6. The effectiveness of utilizing community resources will be increased by incorporating provision for them in the course of study.
7. The effectiveness of each experience should be evaluated in regard to both the learning outcomes and the administrative planning and organization.
8. An inventory of all material and human resources should be made and an up-to-date file kept.
9. Groups should be kept small enough for effective instruction.

10. Teachers should study the resources in advance.
11. Arrangements should be carefully made to insure safety on trips.
12. Necessary permission should be secured, and pupils should be instructed in proper conduct.
13. A community project or activity should be integrated with the work of the classroom.
14. The teacher has the obligation to understand the people and the community in which he works.
15. Community service projects should help solve problems, not create them.

Proposed Advantages *With which ones do you agree?*

1. Study trips give students direct experience with their environment and make them sensitive to it.
2. Contacts with reality give meaning to abstract ideas and theories.
3. Visits in the community or presentations at school open doors to career possibilities.
4. Pleasurable experiences with the concrete increase motivation for further study and increased retention.
5. A community is a large and functional laboratory of human interaction, production and consumption, services, and natural and man-made phenomena of all kinds—a laboratory unreproducible even at a fantastic cost.
6. Contacts between school and community improve public support of education.
7. Field trips bring country children to the city and city children to the country.
8. Valuable and inexpensive specimens can be secured right in the community.
9. Some nonschool agencies can teach many things more effectively than the school.
10. Teachers are benefited by gaining a better understanding of the culture of the community, the people with whom they work, and new sources of teaching aids.
11. Study of the community promotes understanding and cooperation among individuals and groups of different interests and backgrounds, including the pupil's peers.
12. Appreciation is developed for the contribution made by all groups in the community.
13. The problems and needs of different agencies and officials are brought to light.

14. Attitudes are more readily changed and prejudices more easily broken down by face-to-face experience.
15. Work in the community studies democracy at work—its values, needs, and processes.
16. Experience in cooperative planning, cooperative work, and cooperative evaluation is made possible.
17. Pride in one's community and neighbors develops.
18. Often people have not seen things in their own community which visitors travel long distances to see.
19. Study trips teach children how to explore, observe, investigate, and share direct personal experiences with others.
20. Every community has retired people of unique talent who can bring valuable benefits to school children. They may range from retired legislators to artists and entertainers.
21. Actually study trips can be begun with little expense; they may be as simple as taking a walk to study the trees or rocks on the school grounds.
22. Parents often benefit from being involved in study trips or panel discussions at the school.

Criticisms and Difficulties to Be Anticipated *Do you agree?*

1. Some phases of community life are too sensitive to welcome close scrutiny and study by students. Social, labor, racial, political, and business segments of the community may not want to be subjects of investigation and analysis.
2. Most field trips are a waste of time because they accomplish little that could not be achieved in another way.
3. Teachers are conditioned to think that significant learning takes place only within the four walls of the classroom.
4. Teachers are dedicated to the idea that textbooks and learning are synonymous.
5. A successful program is very difficult to implement if the administration of the school is skeptical or fails to provide leadership.
6. Field trips lack intellectual substance.
7. Responsibility and liability of teachers is too great.
8. Taking care of a myriad of necessary details becomes extremely burdensome.
9. Most field experiences are too costly.
10. Utilizing community resources requires time disproportionate to their value.

Summary Assessment

Changes in the lives of young people during the past few years have been real and deep. Their search for a new life style has grown out of a basic change in values, and their lack of commitment to the value system of the past has disturbed their elders. Their dissatisfaction with the present program of education has been demonstrated by vandalism in school buildings, disrespect for teachers and administrators, necessity for police officers in school corridors and classrooms, and rebellion on the campuses of colleges and high schools.

The relevance of education to the lives of individuals and the problems and needs of society have come under serious question. Perhaps the schools have lost touch with the real world beyond their walls. Only by moving out into the vast laboratories of our complex social and industrial life can education give increased meaning and purpose to classroom instruction.

The community is a boundless multi-media center — an unreproducible laboratory of human interaction; a huge storehouse of enjoyment, problems, challenges, and opportunities. To the people who live there, work there, play there, and rear their families there, it should be a source of concern, security, hope, and pride. Youth too, should find it so.

Fuller understanding of the problems of society and involvement in their solution will help students in shaping their values, building their loyalties, and developing perspective. Young people of eighteen will be able to vote intelligently only if they have had many opportunities to observe and work with real life problems. To this end, the full utilization of community resorces is not only an aid; it is an urgent necessity.

A Few Leaders in the Movement

John Bremer
Bertis E. Capehart
James Giddis
Kenneth Glass
Lyal E. Holder
David Hugo
Ronald B. Jackson
Herbert Otto
Thomas Webb

A Few Places Where the Innovation Is Used

Arlington County, Va.
Butler, Pa.
Fall River, Mass.
Hickory, N.C.
Kokomo, Ind.
Middletown, Ohio
Philadelphia, Pa.
Tacoma, Wash.
Wyandotte, Mich.

Bibliography

Clancy, Peter M. and Milton A. Gabrielson, eds., "A Report of First National Community School Clinic," *The Journal of Educational Sociology*, XXIII, No. 4 (1959), entire issue.

Cory, Kenneth E., "Using Local Resources in Developing Geography Concepts and Understandings," *Social Education*, XXX, No. 12 (1966), 617-620.

Hirsch, Bennett, "Living Laboratories Aid Science," *The Instructor*, LXXV, No. 10 (1966), 32-33.

Jackson, Ronald B., "Schools and Communities: A Necessary Relevance," *The Clearing House*, XLIV, No. 8 (1970), 488-490.

Kenough, Jean, "Updating Community Helper Projects," *The Instructor*, LXXV, No. 9 (1966), 54, 102.

Lacattiva, Claire A., "Selected Supervisory Practices in the Use of Community Resources," *Journal of Educational Research*, LX, No. 3 (1966), 139-141.

Marcus, Robert, Edward Bispo, and Irving Catuna, "Cultural Profiles for All . . . ," *National Association of Secondary School Principals*, LI, No. 316 (1967), 91-99.

Olsen, Edward G., ed., *The School and Community Reader*. New York: Macmillan, 1963.

Rolser, Thomas, "How Industry Can Aid Inner-City Education," *Catholic School Journal*, LXIX, No. 6 (1969), 21-22.

Roth, Marjorie L., "Resource File," *The Instructor*, LXXVIII, No. 1 (1968), 41.

Staley, Frederick A., "Community Resources, the Forgotten World of Knowledge." *Educational Screen and Audiovisual Guide*, XLIV, No. 3 (1965), 27.

Street, David, ed., *Innovation in Mass Education*, pp. 145-176. New York: Wiley, 1969.

Weatherford, I.W., "Using Community Resources," *Business Education Forum*, XXI, No. 7 (1967), 11-13.

Wiman, Raymond V., *Instructional Materials*. Worthington, Ohio: Charles A. Jones, 1972.

Wright, Elizabeth Atwell, *Educating for Diversity*. New York: John Day, 1965.

Sex Education and Family Living 17

Definition

Sex education and family living is that component of the instructional program that attempts to enable the child to develop understanding of the physical, emotional, social, and spiritual nature of sexuality. It recognizes that sex is the basis of reproduction and continuity for all life, and that males and females have different, but equally important, roles in the home and community. These roles complement one another. They provide for the richest fulfillment of the individual, the family, and society as a whole. Love, respect, security, and happiness in general are built upon an understanding of these roles and the attitudes that prevail relative to persons of the opposite sex.

Starting in the home and early grades, the program deals primarily with general concerns of children such as the origin of life, differences in male and female appearances, and social roles. With the approach of adolescence, physiological changes and functions receive increased attention. How emotions are aroused and controlled is given more thoughtful consideration. Respect for others and limits of social relationships become significant and legitimate concerns. Family relationships and love of parents and children become matters of continuing importance.

Even if he wishes to, no teacher can avoid teaching sex. Just as sex is indispensable for life, it is an integral part of life for boys and girls in the school as well as in the home. Inservice education can enable teachers in the lower grades to handle problems and questions of sex indirectly as they arise. The high school years may demand a more sophisticated approach and more formal instruction, best achieved through multi-disciplinary efforts involving teachers from many fields, counselors, doctors, nurses, clergymen, social workers, and other members of the community.

Significant Components *Which are essential?*

1. Sex education should extend from infancy through adulthood, the nursery school through college.
2. The purposes of the program must be clearly established before proceeding.
3. Instruction should be individualized to provide for the varying interests and maturity levels of pupils.
4. Particularly in the elementary school, sex education is best integrated with other subjects.
5. Attention must be directed toward strengthening positive attitudes that the child brings from home and changing negative ones.
6. An open climate and an understanding teacher are all-important.
7. Answers should be honest and direct, not going beyond what the child wants or needs to know.
8. Counseling should be provided to assist parents in dealing effectively with the problems of their children.
9. Special provision must be made for children from different socioeconomic and ethnic backgrounds.
10. Dignified and precise vocabulary should be developed.
11. Materials should be carefully pre-studied by the teacher, and they must exercise prudence and good sense.
12. Sex education must not be equated with "giving them the facts of life."
13. A sex education program must not be allowed to deteriorate into a consideration only of menstruation, intercourse, illegitimate pregnancy, and venereal disease.
14. Many resource people including counselors, doctors, nurses, clergymen, social workers, and other members of the community should be utilized in planning and carrying out a program.
15. Careful and continuing evaluation of the program and its results is essential.
16. Sex must be recognized and accepted as a natural, normal part of life.
17. It must be recognized, too, that the misuse of sex can be extremely detrimental to emotional and physical health.

18. New concepts should be introduced only as warranted by the maturity level and social problems that confront or are likely to confront the child.
19. Teachers must be alert to opportunities for indirect teaching since this is more effective than direct instruction.

Proposed Advantages *With which ones do you agree?*

1. Sex education helps children find their way through happy adolescence to satisfying and effective adulthood.
2. Insights for formulating sound values are developed.
3. The home as the center of the child's world is enhanced.
4. Sex education extends the cooperative efforts of the home and the school and deemphasizes the influences of the street in providing information and shaping attitudes.
5. Future parents will be better equipped to deal with the problems of their children.
6. Sex education assists in bridging the generation gap by helping youth to identify with and understand adults.
7. Youth are encouraged to treat one another with love, respect, and consideration.
8. An understanding of parental love and care is fostered.
9. If emotional pressures and physiological changes are understood as normal functions, unwarranted fears and anxieties are reduced.
10. The probability of success and dignity in adult life is increased.
11. Sex education decreases promiscuity and illegitimacy.
12. The incidence of venereal disease is reduced.
13. Guidelines and limits of conduct are established for thoughtful use of increasing independence.
14. Sex education helps married couples to avoid and resolve conflict through increased understanding of physical, emotional and psychological differences.
15. Although physical attraction is recognized and accepted as a real factor in love, deeper and more comprehensive meanings of self and of sexuality are discovered through an adequate educational program.
16. The child sees the process of human reproduction as it relates to plants and other animals and to the perpetuation of life.

Criticisms and Difficulties to Be Anticipated *Do you agree?*

1. Sex education and family living is a very personal matter and belongs in the home and the church.

2. The schools are continually assuming roles inconsistent with, and in neglect of, their primary responsibilities.
3. Mass education is ineffective in dealing with matters as personal as sex education and family living.
4. Bringing sex relations to the attention of children arouses unnecessary curiosity and anxiety.
5. Sexuality and sex should not be reduced to a science.
6. Sex education promotes experimentation and promiscuity.
7. Much of the text material used is produced primarily for its sensational appeal and is very "raw."
8. The stability and maturity of teachers who are constantly dwelling on sex are open to serious question.
9. Since sex education came into the schools, the record of promiscuity, drugs, venereal diseases, and illegitimacy has been pitiful indeed.
10. Teaching attitudes and values is not education; it is indoctrination.
11. Students may take the discussions far afield and pervert the purpose of the instruction.
12. Mass media and producers of pornographic material capitalize on the interest and curiosity generated in children by the schools.
13. Lasting attitudes toward sex and family living are established long before children come to school.
14. Prudishness of teachers, their own uncertain attitudes, and their insurmountable prejudices create frustration, anxieties, and fears.
15. Children can learn all they need to know about sex in a very short time.
16. Sex education "demoralizes" young people and violates every principle of decency and good taste.
17. Advocates of sex education are really Marxists in disguise.

Summary Assessment

Instruction in sex education and family living is not new. It has long been a concern in the junior and senior high schools, but the realization that it must receive continuous attention at all levels is of more recent origin. The mobility of our population, congestion and anonymity of large cities, poverty, affluence, and the impact of a multitude of frustrations and tensions have caused a reassessment of conventional mores, values, and patterns of behavior. The decreasing influence of the home, coupled with the changing roles of the church, has quickened the search for new solutions to the ever-present problems of young people.

There appears to be general agreement that teaching sex education and family living is important, even crucial, for the individual, the home, and society. If love, concern, and emotional stability are not developed in the home, other agencies must share the responsibility. Community education for premarriage couples and for parents holds promise. There appears to be an increasing realization that the marriage ceremony may be the beginning of a happy and satisfying married life or a prelude to misery.

Who should teach sex education and family living, how it should be taught, and what aspects should be stressed, have recently become matters of heated controversy. The public flare-ups of the last few years have perhaps been the result of poorly conceived programs, misplaced emphases, ineptness and indiscretion on the part of some teachers, unduly sensational materials, misunderstandings, and unwillingness on the part of certain individuals and groups to face the needs of youth and society squarely and realistically.

Despite agreement on high-sounding objectives, too many programs have emphasized only negative approaches. Copulation, masturbation, menstruation, contraception, reproductive organs, illegitimacy, and venereal diseases constitute the entire content of some programs. Little wonder, then, that they arouse vehement objections. Educators must stop looking at sex education as a way of teaching "the facts of life" and address themselves to all the emotional, psychological, physical, and spiritual factors that contribute to vital and successful living. In a positive sense, sex education is character education; and that must be a vital concern of all groups, not of a single agency. Serious mistakes make the concerns of parents legitimate, but people of good intentions must not obstruct progress through emotional controversy.

As Carl Fehrle puts it, "Sex created the family. Proper sex education can preserve the family."*

A Few Leaders in the Movement

American Medical Assn.	Stanley Fowler	Adeline Levin
Mary S. Calderone	Lester Kirkendall	Frederick Margolis
Gordon Drake	Carl Knutson	SIECUS

*Carl C. Fehrle, "The Natural Birth of Sex Education," *Educational Leadership*, XXVII, No. 6 (1970), 577.

A Few Places Where the Innovation Is Used

Anaheim, Calif.
Atlanta, Ga.
Dallas, Tex.
Evanston, Ill.
Flint, Mich.
Kansas City, Mo.
Mamaroneck, N.Y.
St. Louis, Mo.
Washington, D.C.

Bibliography

Abramson, Paul, ed., "Sex Education: Eight Teachable Moments," *Grade Teacher*, LXXXVI, No. 3 (1968), 65, 121, 122, 128.

Breasted, Mary, *Oh! Sex Education!* New York: Praeger, 1970.

Broderick, Carlfred B. and Jessie Bernard, eds., *The Individual, Sex, and Society*. Baltimore: The Johns Hopkins Press, 1969.

Calderone, Mary S., "Goodbye to the Birds and the Bees," *American Education*, II, No. 10 (1969), 16-22.

———, "Shameful Neglect of Sex Education," *P.T.A. Magazine*, LXI, No. 9 (1967), 4-7.

Dale, Gayle and George C. Chamis, *Sex Education Guide for Teachers*. Flint, Mich.: Flint Public Schools, 1968.

Ellis, Albert and Albert Abarbanel, *The Encyclopedia of Sexual Behavior* (2 vols.). New York: Hawthorne, 1961.

Fehrle, Carl C., "The Natural Birth of Sex Education," *Educational Leadership*, XXVII, No. 6 (1970), 573-577.

Goodheart, Barbara, "Sex in the Schools: Education or Titillation?" *Today's Health*, XLVIII, No. 2 (1970), 28-30, 76, 79-80, 83-85.

Greenberg, Herbert M., *Teaching with Feeling*, pp. 177-186. Toronto: Macmillan, 1969.

Inlow, Gail M., *The Emergent In Curriculum*, pp. 212-234. New York: Wiley, 1966.

Juhasz, Anne McCreary, "Background Factors, Extent of Sex Knowledge and Source of Information," *The Journal of School Health*, XXXIX, No. 1 (1969), 32-39.

Kilander, Holger F., *Sex Education in the Schools*. Toronto: Macmillan, 1970.

Kirkendall, Lester A., "Sex Education: Blunt Answers for Tough Questions," *Reader's Digest*, XCII, No. 554 (1968), 80-84.

McCary, James L., *Human Sexuality*. New York: Van Nostrand Reinhold, 1967.

N.A.I.S. Institute on Sex Education, *Sex Education and the Schools*. New York: Harper, 1966.

Rowan, Carl T. and David M. Mazie, "Sex Education: Powder Keg in Our Schools," *Reader's Digest*, XCV, No. 570 (1969), 73-78.

"Sex Education: How It Is Being Taught In Elementary Classrooms," *Grade Teacher*, LXXXIV, No. 9 (1967), 122-125, 172-173.

Perceptual-Motor Learning 18

Definition

Perceptual-motor learning is the process of developing improved efficiency in body movement through a carefully organized program of learning activities. It is based upon the principle that people develop their native potential through many experiences, one of which is perceptual-motor learning. Body control, body image, self-concept, social adjustment, academic learning, emotional stability, and general personality can be improved through perceptual-motor training. How the child assesses his abilities within the total context of self and environment is considered a significant aspect of his self-concept and his interaction with other people, objects, and experiences.

Although perceptual-motor learning is recognized as valuable for all children, it seems to be particularly beneficial for the neurologically impaired, physically handicapped, hyperactive, mentally retarded, and emotionally disturbed. Children with these deficiencies constitute about 10 to 15 per cent of the school population. The instructional program is designed to enhance body-image, awareness of time, spatial judgment, and movement control.

Differentiation of body parts and functions, laterality, reaction time, balance, locomotion, manual dexterity, strength and endurance, agility, visual fixation and mobility, and auditory skills are among the functions included in the program. Among the learning activities are crawling, walking lines or balance beams, metronomic pacing, relaxation exercises, rhythmic games, skipping, chalkboard exercises, hopping into squares or circles, throwing, catching, grasping, drawing, and writing. The work is done in classrooms, gymnasiums, and clinics.

Incorporated in the program are activities for improvement in general performance and those designed for development of specific skills. The relationship between motor development and intellectual learning is emphasized. Perceptual manipulation of real things is considered essential for building a foundation for meaningful symbolic perception needed in classroom learning. The perceptual relationships are extracted from the various motor experiences and serve as a basis for perceiving new relationships in such areas as reading, writing, arithmetic, spelling, and handwork.

Significant Components *Which are essential?*

1. Perceptual-motor programs should be based on sound principles of child development and of learning.
2. In order to prevent raising unwarranted hopes on the part of parents, claims for the program should, whenever possible, be based on scientific research.
3. Early identification and treatment is very important.
4. All those concerned must realize that deficiencies are not of the child's making and are subject to remediation, especially if recognized and dealt with early.
5. Instruction should start at a low level and move forward in a developmental progression.
6. At the outset comprehensive examination of the pupil's physical, mental, and emotional functioning is indispensable.
7. Motor-perception should be treated as part of a total instructional program.
8. Competent teachers with some special training, who understand many aspects of learning, are needed.
9. Teachers should work closely with doctors, psychologists, and other specialists.
10. Wherever possible, a well qualified team assures maximum success.
11. Some special equipment is necessary.
12. The program must not be looked upon as a panacea for all motor, academic. and behavioral problems.

13. More than in most areas of learning, special attention should be given to readiness and transfer of training.
14. Basic in the program are learning activities designed to improve differentiation and integration of the movements of the different body parts.
15. Pupils must be free from social pressure, criticism, and threat.
16. Special training should be provided in relaxation and impulse control to relieve tensions and alleviate disruptive behavior.
17. Observations and suggestions of parents and the regular classroom teacher should be invited and carefully considered.

Proposed Advantages

With which ones do you agree?

1. Relieving problems of movement allows the pupil to concentrate on the experience or task itself, rather than on the locomotor obstacles.
2. Early motor learning improves total development as well as movement efficiency.
3. Cognitive learning, such as perceiving printed symbols, benefits from improvement in perception.
4. The attention span is lengthened, especially in the case of the hyperactive pupil.
5. Functioning of the central nervous system is improved if appropriate motor activities are practiced.
6. Perceptual-motor learning is important for emotional development and effective emotional functioning.
7. Ability to participate in games and other physical activities improves the self-concept of the child.
8. The child is assisted in building those readiness skills that help him to achieve in academic areas such as reading, writing, arithmetic, and spelling.
9. Motor improvement develops independence, self-confidence, and willingness to try.
10. Improving visual-manual skills relieves tensions and anxieties resulting from inability to perform many tasks.
11. Improvement in a child's motor functions improves his social relations with his peers.
12. Children are taught to see relationships and arrange components of a situation in a specific order.
13. In the overactive child, it develops self-control.
14. Improved movement is significant because others readily observe the child's movement and judge him by it.

15. Tensions are relieved through vigorous movements.
16. The relief of emotional problems facilitates greater success in the classroom.
17. Unity and wholeness of the child's life is enhanced by his awareness of his relationship with objects in his environment.
18. Individual movements are combined into patterns, many of which become automatic.
19. Ability to handle himself more efficiently is significant for the child's safety.
20. The child's capabilities for exploring, manipulating, and securing different kinds of information are increased.

Criticisms and Difficulties to Be Anticipated *Do you agree?*

1. Concern and anxiety of parents and teachers may present problems different from those encountered when working with normal children and may compound the child's problem.
2. Facilities for diagnosis and help in special areas may be inadequate.
3. Teachers may try various approaches without having sound, verified reasons for using them.
4. Concerned parents may be misled and disillusioned by those who hold out false hopes.
5. Unscrupulous individuals take advantage of families that have children with marked deficiencies.
6. Some people imply that motor activities affect the central nervous system directly.
7. Requiring pupils to engage in motor activities in which they have marked deficiency frustrates and destroys self-confidence.
8. Competent personnel for conducting the work is not available.
9. There is a lack of tested knowledge to determine the activities that are appropriate for particular deficiencies.
10. The fact that the child who is atypical in body movement is usually deficient in other areas complicates diagnosis and treatment.
11. Teachers, parents, and administrators often do not understand the purpose and nature of the program.
12. Progress requires patience and a long period of time, and results are often difficult to identify.
13. If pupils are threatened or punished, adverse effects are likely to result.

Summary Assessment

Perceptual-motor learning has spread significantly during the past decade as educators have become increasingly aware of the significance of instruction in motor efficiency. They have come to recognize its potential for furthering perceptual awareness and for helping deficient children with reading, writing, spelling, arithmetic, and other classroom pursuits. There is considerable evidence indicating that perception improved through motor training releases latent potential and enhances intellectual performance. The conflict between those who believe in specificity or perceptual-motor skills and those who stress generality and transfer in performance seems to be subsiding.

The value of carefully planned motor activities for hyperactive and emotionally disturbed children is receiving increased attention. There is also evidence of the usefulness of movement training in helping normal children with a variety of learning difficulties. Significant, too, is the recent emphasis on enhancing the self-concept and improving social adjustment of the handicapped.

Many aspects of the functioning of motor systems as well as the operation of perceptual processes are not yet understood. However, researchers in neurology, physiology, psychology, optometry, medicine, and physical education are engaged in serious and productive study. Additional research is needed concerning the nature and causes of deficiencies and the kinds of motor and other experiences that are needed to relieve specific motor disabilities and to improve performance in other areas of classroom learning. Increasingly, the outcomes of systematic investigations report positive results. Progress to date and the growing interest in the field give promise of increasing help from perceptual-motor learning for both teachers and pupils. If the number of children needing help are to receive it, the schools must make the necessary curricular provisions because private practitioners and clinics cannot handle the large load.

A Few Leaders in the Movement

Ray H. Barsch
Arthur Benton
H. J. Birch
Robert Boger
Bryant Cratty
Carl H. Delacato
Glenn Doman
Marianne Frostig
G. N. Getman
Newell C. Kephart
James J. McCarthy
Douglas Wiseman

A Few Places Where the Innovation Is Used

Columbus, Ohio	Philadelphia, Pa.	Tucson, Ariz.
Colo. State Univ.	Purdue Univ.	University of Wis.
Dayton, Ohio	St. Paul, Minn.	Winter Haven, Fla.
Madison, Wis.	Seattle, Wash.	
Miami Univ.	Somerset, Ky.	

Bibliography

Barsch, Ray H., *Achieving Perceptual-Motor Efficiency: A Space-Oriented Approach to Learning*. Volume 1 of a Perceptual-Motor Curriculum. Seattle: Special Child Publications, 1967.

———, *Enriching Perception and Cognition: Techniques for Teachers*. Volume 2 of a Perceptual-Motor Curriculum. Seattle: Special Child Publications, 1968.

Chaney, Clara M. and Newell C. Kephart, *Motoric Aids to Perceptual Training*. Columbus, Ohio: Merrill, 1968.

Cratty, Bryant J., *Perceptual-Motor Behavior and Educational Processes*. Springfield, Ill.: Thomas, 1969.

Cratty, Bryant J. and Sr. Margaret Mary Martin, *Perceptual-Motor Efficiency in Children*. Philadelphia: Lea and Febiger, 1969.

Cratty, Bryant J., and Leon Whisell, *Perceptual-Motor Behavior and Educational Processes*. Springfield, Ill.: Thomas, 1969.

Dillon, Edward J., Earl J. Heath, and Carroll W. Biggs, *Comprehensive Programming For Success In Learning*. Columbus, Ohio: Merrill, 1970.

Frierson, Edward C. and Walter B. Barbe, eds., *Educating Children With Learning Disabilities*. New York: Appleton-Century-Crofts, 1967.

Getman, G. N. and Elmer R. Kane, "The Physiology of Readiness," (An action program for the development of perception for children.) Minneapolis: P.A.S.S., 1964.

International Approach to Learning Disabilities of Children and Youth. Third Annual International Conference, Tulsa, Okla., 1966. Tulsa: The Association for Children with Learning Disabilities, 1967.

Johnson, Doris J. and Helmer R. Myklebust, *Learning Disabilities*. New York: Grune and Stratton, 1967.

McCarthy, James J. and Joan F., *Learning Disabilities*. Boston: Allyn and Bacon, 1969.

Otto, Wayne and Karl Koenke, eds., *Remedial Teaching*. Boston: Houghton Mifflin, 1969.

Otto, Wayne and Richard A. McMenemy, *Corrective and Remedial Teaching*. Boston: Houghton Mifflin, 1966.

Simpson, Dorothy M., *Learning to Learn*. Columbus, Ohio: Merrill, 1968.

Sutphin, Florence E. and Charles W. McQuarrie, *A Perceptual Testing-Training Handbook for First Grade Teachers*. Winter Haven, Fla.: Boyd Brothers, 1967.

Part Four

Reorganization for Better Learning

Community School 19

Definition

A community school is a school whose educational program grows out of the life of the community and serves to improve that life. Through mobilizing all available human and other resources, it becomes a center of vital learning and of many varied opportunities. It is a unifying force for community services directed toward improving the living of individuals and groups, as well as a life-centered educational institution designed to develop mature, productive citizens.

Two closely related, yet somewhat different, approaches are included within the school-community partnership. The one focuses upon the regular school program for children and youth, advocating a school where learning and living join hands. The school program moves out into the community for its learning experiences, establishes relevance of learning exercises, and pursues the principle of purposeful learning by doing. Community resources and action projects provide rich opportunities for education and at the same time assist in solving individual and group problems. The community serves as a learning laboratory for school youth, and the school offers leadership for improving the life of the citizenry.

The other concept of community education emphasizes building an education-centered community through opening the schools to people of all ages from early morning until late at night on an all-week, year-round schedule. The offerings are determined by the needs and interests of the people and include everything from literacy programs and creative writing to sports and weight-watching. Multi-media centers, swimming pools, laboratories, health facilities, art rooms, and centers for the aging are open to all who want to use them. The schools are centers of neighborhood and community life. Participation in sclf-government, health services, social and recreational activities, continuous study, and community improvement is stressed. Frequently, special attention is directed toward strengthening the ability of lower socioeconomic groups to improve their living. Opportunities are provided for upgrading vocational competencies, attacking problems of crime and drugs, securing personal and legal counseling, improving home management, building better social relations, and expanding recreational interests.

By involving youth in learning and working in the community and by bringing all citizens into the schools, people of all ages and of divergent social and economic backgrounds learn to work together for the improvement of themselves, their families, and their communities.

Significant Components — *Which are essential?*

1. The community school must have concern for and provide services for all socioeconomic levels and ages.
2. The curriculum and services of the school must evolve out of the interests, problems, and needs of the community.
3. All segments of the community must be involved in planning, carrying out, and evaluating the program.
4. Educational opportunities and services must be available from early morning until late evening, all week throughout the year.
5. The school must be a center of community life, and its program must be life-centered.
6. Services must be available at the neighborhood level.
7. The community school should be under a single board of education and a single administrative staff and be well financed.
8. It must proceed on the philosophy that there is a great deal more to education than intellectualism.
9. It must operate as a service center to meet the health, recreational, social, economic, and other needs of the people.
10. The community school must have a well-trained, competent community services director, who understands the community

in which he is working, and a lay as well as a professional staff that is thoroughly committed to the philosophy of the community school and has competence in developing a life-centered program.

11. The community school must be flexible enough to accommodate an infinite variety of changing interests and demands.
12. Support from all segments of the community is needed: clubs, social agencies, governmental divisions, churches, board of education, and political leadership.
13. New buildings should be designed so that certain parts can be used independently of the rest of the building, and the cost of maintenance and supervision can be minimized.

Proposed Advantages *With which ones do you agree?*

1. The community school stresses the concept that a person's education depends upon the totality of his life; and the quality of his life depends upon education.
2. Low-income people and others build self-respect, self-confidence, and self-reliance through practice in developing political and social skills and participation in decision-making.
3. The community school builds a feeling of attachment to and pride in the community on the part of people from all economic levels.
4. Participation in school planning fosters a feeling of responsibility for assisting with such problems as student strikes, vandalism, drugs, truancy, and other forms of delinquency.
5. Since children can hardly have a positive self-image if their parents do not, educating parents is essential for effective education of children.
6. The tendency of teachers to blame the home for many of the children's deficiencies is reduced through developing a feeling of partnership between teachers and parents in the education of the young.
7. Economy is effected through the elimination of needless duplication of facilities, administration, and services.
8. Interest, significance, and purpose are brought into the lives of aging citizens.
9. Business and industry benefit from more competent, stable, and satisfied personnel.
10. A sense of personal responsibility and self-reliance strengthens government at the local level.
11. Citizens are given the opportunity to meet the continuous demands of change and discover new talents.
12. Working together at all ages on problems significant to all bridges the gap between youth and their elders.

13. Adults learn to read and write, new mothers learn to care for their families.
14. People of all racial and social groups learn to understand and respect one another by working and playing together.
15. Community projects develop leadership and followership.
16. The traditional verbalism of the classroom is impugned.
17. Community schools help alleviate the impersonal ills of urbanization by integrating and unifying the neighborhood.
18. Community schools provide a vehicle for attacking illiteracy, poverty, disease, and unemployment.
19. The survival and strength of democracy are assured by the fullest development of all human resources.

Criticisms and Difficulties to Be Anticipated *Do you agree?*

1. A good community-school program is excessively costly.
2. Few teachers have the orientation, dedication, or skills needed to conduct an effective program.
3. It is very difficult to involve low-income people in a community-school program.
4. It is also difficult to secure the support of community leaders and organizations.
5. Most of the services included in the program are not the legitimate function of the school.
6. Education and services for adults are sure to decrease the funds available for educating children and youth.
7. The community-school concept implies a planned society, inimical to our heritage of freedom.
8. Involvement in many different activities will cause the schools to lose sight of their responsibility for intellectual excellence.
9. A community school presents too many diverse problems to be handled expertly by one agency.
10. Adults are difficult to involve in constructive programs and quickly lose interest.
11. Activities planned by lay people usually degenerate into trivia.
12. Use of school facilities by teachers during off-school hours is likely to result in conflict with teachers and administrators in the day school.
13. Transportation and liability are real problems.
14. The community school takes support away from clubs, churches, and other organizations in the community.
15. Socialistic ventures of this kind destroy private initiative.

Summary Assessment

The community-school concept embraces two aspects. One relates to a life-centered educational program for pupils in the elementary and secondary schools, involving them in the utilization of community resources and in learning experiences centering around the solution of meaningful community problems. The other directs major emphasis to continuing education for all citizens and to providing services for enriching the life of the individual and the community.

The former seems to be a natural extension of educational opportunity for youth, consistent with the school's responsibility for making its program vital and relevant and for discharging its obligation to the society that supports it. The need to add realism and motivational power to conventional school experiences by moving out of the walls of the classrooms into the challenging laboratories of life has long been recognized. However, little more than lip service has been given to the idea.

Extended education and services to all citizens are brought into focus by the rapidly increasing complexities and problems of urban society. The mobility of population, demands for new skills, and the breakdown in family and community life add urgency to the search for new solutions. Poverty, drug addiction, pollution, and crime cry out for help. There are those who insist that the time is past due when the school must become a truly social institution. They believe that only through active participation in decision-making can adults as well as youth build a positive self-concept and escape alienation. Those who have thought of education as a need only for young people are beginning to wonder if we should invest all our educational resources in one age group.

In the community school there is no "before school" or "after school," there is no "new school year," there is no age limit for attendance. Basic tools of learning, home membership, citizenship, vocational skills, recreational and social experiences for all segments of the population contribute to enhancing the life of each individual and to improving the total community. New goals, ideals, values, and hopes are fostered. Educators give their professional know-how and leadership to making the school the catalytic agent for building cohesiveness and unity of purpose throughout the community.

The time has come when schools must go to the streets to help people help themselves. This can be accomplished if citizens are ready to provide the resources for schools and community to join forces and march forward to a brighter future.

A Few Leaders in the Movement

John Bremer	Ernest Melby	Maurice Seay
Daniel Levine	Charles Stewart Mott	Mark Shedd
Frank J. Manley	Harding Mott	James Showkeir
Robert Marcus	Edward G. Olsen	W. Fred Totten

A Few Places Where the Innovation Is Used

Alpena, Mich.	Flint, Mich.	San Jose State College
Atlanta, Ga.	Fla. Atlantic Univ.	Springfield, Ohio
Dade County, Fla.	Monterey, Calif.	Tipp City, Ohio
E. Baton Rouge, La.	New Haven, Conn.	W. Mich. Univ.

Bibliography

Carmichael, Benjamin E. and Nita Nardo, "Emerging Patterns in Community-Centered Schools," *Childhood Education*, XLIII, No. 6 (1967), 319-323.

Cordasco, Francesco, "Urban Education—Leonard Covello and the Community School," *School and Society*, XCVIII, No. 2326 (1970), 298-299.

Cox, Donald W. and Liza Lazorko, "A School Without Walls: A City for a Classroom," *Nation's Schools*, LXXXIV, No. 3 (1969), 51-54.

Greenberg, James and Robert E. Roush, "A Visit to the School Without Walls: Two Impressions," *Phi Delta Kappan*, LI, No. 9 (1970), 480-484.

Herman, Barry E., "Winchester Community School: A Laboratory of Ideas," *Educational Leadership*, XXV, No. 4 (1968), 341-343.

Howard, W. Hickey and Curtis Van Vorhees, eds., *The Role of the School in Community Education*. Midland, Mich.: Pendell, 1969.

Jackson, Ronald B., "Schools and Communities: A Necessary Relevance," *The Clearing House*, XLIV, No. 8 (1970), 488-490.

Lanning, Frank and Wesley A. Many, eds., *Basic Education for the Disadvantaged Adult: Theory and Practice*. Boston: Houghton Mifflin, 1966.

Levine, Daniel U., "The Community School in Contemporary Perspective," *Elementary School Journal*, LXIX, No. 7 (1968), 109-117.

———, "The Community School in Historical Perspective," *Elementary School Journal*, LXVII, No. 4 (1967), 192-195.

Melby, Ernest O., "The Community-Centered School," *Childhood Education*, XLIII, No. 6 (1967), 316-318.

Olsen, Edward G., ed., *The School and Community Reader*. New York: Macmillan, 1963.

Thatcher, John H., ed., *Public School Adult Education*. Washington, D.C.: National Association of Public School Adult Educators, 1963.

Totten, W. Fred and Frank J. Manley, *The Community School: Basic Concepts, Function, and Organization*. Galien, Mich.: Allied Educational Council, 1969.

The Middle School 20

Definition

In essence the middle school is not an organizational pattern for administrative convenience. It is an idea, a philosophy, to provide a unique educational program to shape the learning pattern of a unique group of children. Typically it encompasses the work of the traditional sixth, seventh, and eighth grades. Often the fifth grade is included; infrequently the ninth grade is part of the school.

It is designed as a school for pupils between elementary and high school and specifically strives to serve the needs of older children, preadolescents, and early adolescents, between 10 and 14. It is usually housed in a separate building, ideally in facilities specially designed for its purposes. The program emphasizes continuous progress, individualization of instruction, and team teaching. The development of self-reliance by placing increased responsibility for learning upon the student is a significant feature. The teacher's role is that of stimulator, guide, and director of learning. Ann Grooms emphasizes this role when she says:

> The middle school teacher is not teaching math; he is not teaching Mary; he is not teaching math to Mary. He is providing support so that she can learn math.*

*Grooms, M. Ann, *Perspectives on the Middle School* (Columbus, Ohio: Charles E. Merrill Publishing Company, 1967), p. 51.

Significant Components *Which are essential?*

1. The purposes and goals must be clearly stated.
2. Teachers who are committed to the philosophy and purposes of the middle school must be selected and developed.
3. Teachers must have competence in counseling as well as in specific subject areas.
4. Promoting understanding of the purposes of and a positive attitude toward the program on the part of pupils and parents is important.
5. The resource center must contain varied and appropriate materials for use in individualized study programs.
6. Activities normally considered extracurricular must be meaningfully integrated into the regular program.
7. Balance must be established between stability and flexibility.
8. Special effort must be made to avoid simply transferring a traditional junior high school program to the middle school.
9. Provision should be made for team teaching.
10. The total program should be a functional entity, capable of providing for the mental, emotional, and physical needs of pupils of this age.
11. Sufficient space must be available to allow for flexible scheduling, freedom of movement, and variation in activities.
12. The program should incorporate the nongraded concept.
13. The school should emphasize self-motivation, independent study, and individual responsibility through personal involvement.
14. The school must give special emphasis to providing a cohesive, but still flexible, link between the primary school and the high school.

Proposed Advantages *With which ones do you agree?*

1. The middle school provides for an integrated program to meet the physical, emotional, and intellectual needs of a unique age group.
2. The philosophy of the middle school avoids miniature high school courses, replacing them with a varied program of its own.
3. A variety of integrated experiences is substituted for such isolated activities as interschool athletics.
4. The program promotes individualization for a student group characterized by great variability.

5. Smooth articulation is provided between the educational experience of childhood and adolescence.
6. The best features of the self-contained program of the primary school and the departmentalized structure of the secondary school are incorporated into the program.
7. The middle school capitalizes on the special talent of teachers to meet the varied needs of individuals and groups.
8. The program emphasizes self-direction and pupil involvement.
9. A good middle school program reduces undesirable pressures on youth.
10. Flexibility in time schedule, freedom of movement, and variation in learning activities are provided for.
11. Interdisciplinary approaches in all subjects are encouraged.
12. A new approach generates interest and motivation on the part of pupils, teachers, administrators, and parents.

Criticisms and Difficulties to Be Anticipated — *Do you agree?*

1. Teachers, pupils, and parents may be oriented to a more traditional approach to the extent that they misunderstand and even reject the philosophy of the middle school.
2. The pattern of the junior high school is likely to persist and thus hinder the development of distinctly new purposes and approaches.
3. The distinct nature and problems of the 10- to 14-year-old may continue to be neglected.
4. Administrative and organizational factors may become the dominant considerations.
5. Lack of adequate space, equipment, and materials may be an obstacle.
6. Teachers may become discouraged because of failure to realize immediate or complete fulfillment of their hopes and aspirations.
7. To some observers, flexibility and freedom may seem like disorganization and confusion.
8. Fragmentation may interfere with unity of learning.
9. In some states, traditional standards and requirements may have to be revised.
10. Existing buildings may require extensive alteration.
11. Excessive attention given to the new unit may be resented by primary and high school staffs.
12. Changes in program and methodology may be introduced too abruptly.

Summary Assessment

The middle school is gradually overcoming one of its early handicaps resulting from misinterpretation of its purposes. In many places, it was instituted merely as a means of accommodating rapidly increasing enrollments by shifting them from one building to another. The middle school is good only as it emerges as a distinct institution with its own objectives and programs designed to serve a segment of the school population that possesses unique characteristics. The failure of the traditional junior high school to serve the needs of its students has been an impetus and an advantage in shaping the new school, although remnants of the previous structure and program persist.

The middle school must not be a miniature high school or an advanced elementary school, but must establish its own identity as an institution capable of meeting the intellectual, personal, social, aesthetic, emotional, and physical problems that confront pre-teen and early teen-age youth. It has made a good beginning toward creating a climate in which it is possible and satisfying for each child to wrestle with the incongruities of life facing him as a result of the pressures, needs, potentialities, and opportunities that confront him. Caution must be exercised to prevent the changes of the middle school from being merely changes in form and organization. New strategies must be accompanied by new, more relevant content and produce new and better results.

Currently, a distinct handicap to realizing the fullest potential of the middle school is the failure of teacher-education institutions to prepare teachers for the new school. Advantages and disadvantages continue. Whether the advantages outweigh the disadvantages depends in large measure upon the support given to the developing ideas and programs, the quality of administrative and supervisory leadership, and the commitment of the teachers. Vision, creativeness, continuous assessment, and readjustment are essential to continued progress.

A Few Leaders in the Movement

William M. Alexander
L. E. Burger
John Corwin
Donald H. Eichhorn
Robert Finley
Nicholas Georgiady
M. Ann Grooms
Alvin Howard
Theodore Moss
Samuel H. Popper
Cyril G. Sargent
Emmett L. Williams

A Few Places Where the Innovation Is Used

Amory, Miss.	Eagle Grove, Iowa	Pleasant Hills, Pa.
Barrington, Ill.	East Lansing, Mich.	Reading, Ohio
Bellingham, Wash.	Goshen, N.Y.	Saginaw, Mich.
Beloit, Wis.	High Springs, Fla.	St. Clair, Pa.
Boulder, Colo.	Midland, Mich.	Sarasota County, Fla.
Centerville, Ohio	Mt. Kisco, N.Y.	Sunbury, Ohio
Cleveland, Ohio	New Haven, Conn.	Tiburon, Calif.

Bibliography

Alexander, William, Emmett L. Williams, Mary Compton, Vynce A. Hines, and Dan Prescott, *The Emergent Middle School.* New York: Holt, 1968.

Batezel, George W., "The Middle School: Philosophy, Program, Organization," *The Clearing House*, XLII, No. 8 (1968), 487-490.

Bough, Max, "Theoretical and Practical Aspects of the Middle School," *The Bulletin of the National Association of Secondary School Principals*, March, 1969.

Curtis, Thomas and Wilma Bidwell, "Rationale for Instruction in the Middle School," *Educational Leadership*, XXVII, No. 6 (1970), 578-581.

Eichhorn, Donald H., *The Middle School.* New York: The Center for Applied Research, 1966.

Grooms, M. Ann, *Perspectives on the Middle School.* Columbus, Ohio: Merrill, 1967.

Howard, Alvin, *Teaching in Middle Schools.* Scranton, Pa.: International, 1968.

Howell, Bruce, "The Middle School—Is It Really Any Better?," *North Central Association Quarterly*, XL, 281-287.

McCarthy, Robert, *How to Organize and Operate an Ungraded Middle School*, Englewood Cliffs, N.J.: Prentice-Hall, 1967.

Mellinger, Morris and John A. Rackauskas, *Quest for Identity*. National Survey of the Middle School 1969-70. Chicago State College, 1970.

Moss, Theodore C., *Middle School.* Boston: Houghton Mifflin, 1969.

Overly, Donald E., John R. Kinghorn, and Richard L. Preston, *Humanizing Education Through the Middle School.* Worthington, Ohio: Charles A. Jones, 1972.

Popper, Samuel H., *The American Middle School.* Waltham, Mass.: Blaisdell, 1967.

"Twenty-Eight Ways to Build Mistakes Out of Your Middle School," *The American School Board Journal*, LVIII, No. 1 (1970), 17-24.

Williams, Emmett L., "What About the Junior High and Middle School?" *The Bulletin of the National Association of Secondary School Principals*, May, 1968.

Wilson, Mildred T. and Samuel H. Popper, "What About the Middle School?" *Today's Education*, LVIII, No. 2 (1969), 52-54.

Courtesy Miami University, Oxford, Ohio

Preschool Education 21

Definition

Preschool education is organized learning experience for children from birth to entrance into the first grade. Frequently the term is applied to children between the ages of three and six. Built on the foundations of Jean Jacques Rousseau, Johann Pestalozzi, and Friedrich Froebel, the theoretical concepts of early childhood education were advanced in this country by G. Stanley Hall, William James, and Arnold Gesell. More recently, Jean Piaget's work on intellectual development has stimulated interest in the education of the very young.

As attention focused upon the deficiencies of economically and socially disadvantaged children, psychological researchers began to warn against the danger of permanent retardation as the price to be paid for neglecting preschoolers from disadvantaged environments. Dramatic increases in I.Q. scores were reported for slum-area children whose experiences were enriched. The launching of the Office of Economic Opportunity's Head Start program in 1965 spurred an almost frantic increase in research and program development.

In many intervention programs, a new emphasis on preparation for academic achievement appeared. In contrast to the free, play-oriented programs of conventional kindergartens and nursery schools, the new approach stresses a highly structured plan to remedy the deficiencies that have been identified. It attempts to discover what areas of learning a child lacks and to provide for them. As a result of this emphasis, the new programs are often looked upon as remedial rather than developmental.

Classes for preschoolers are sponsored by a great variety of agencies, ranging from the federal government to women's clubs. Some programs are well financed, many are conducted on a volunteer basis. Classes, tutoring, and counseling for parents pursue a broad range of objectives and include such functions as health services and instruction for reading and number readiness. Most of the programs are directed toward manipulating the environment of children of the poor and of minority groups in such a way that the pupils will be able to compete more effectively with other children in the academic pursuits of the primary school. Broad and varied experiences are provided to improve perception of the environment, enhance self-concept, and develop new knowledge and skills. All of these, it is hoped, will contribute significantly to intellectual, social, emotional, and physical growth in subsequent years.

Significant Components *Which are essential?*

1. Preschool education should be an integral part of the total school program.
2. The purposes of the program must be understood by all those directly involved and by the general public.
3. Good, attractive physical facilities are especially important for very young children.
4. Competent, well-trained teachers are essential for optimum results.
5. Classes should be kept small.
6. Research findings relating to children, particularly disadvantaged children, should be the basis for establishing objectives and techniques.
7. Pupils and parents should be prepared for the preschool experience, and parental cooperation and participation are important.
8. When the program is focused on the disadvantaged, methods and materials must be appropriate for them.
9. Frequent conferences and meetings with parents should be arranged.

10. The relationship between school and home experiences must be clear.
11. The school and home should capitalize on the diversity of these experiences.
12. The program must offer a wide variety of opportunities for exploring, manipulating, interacting, and inquiring.
13. A free emotional climate should be established that is conducive to security and discovery.
14. A careful balance should be maintained between freedom and responsibility.
15. More research is needed in the areas of program development and evaluation of results.

Proposed Advantages — *With which ones do you agree?*

1. Early experiences are vital for developing a positive self-concept, wholesome attitudes, and healthy relationships with others.
2. Improving the early environment can increase intelligence substantially.
3. By helping the child during his most formative years, preschool education improves his general educability and prepares him for successful school experiences.
4. During the formative years most progress can be made in all aspects of development — physical, intellectual, social, and emotional.
5. Cultural and intellectual deprivation can be overcome, thus preventing permanent retardation.
6. Many diseases, physical handicaps, neurological disorders, and nutritional deficiences can be discovered early.
7. By providing a background of common experience, preschool education helps to close the gap between disadvantaged and advantaged children.
8. Deviant behavior resulting from poor home environment is corrected or alleviated.
9. Early education provides a setting for developing tolerance for frustration.
10. Preschool education is a great aid in developing language and communication skills and in furthering reading and number readiness.
11. A foundation is laid for enjoying the subsequent years of school by having the child become accustomed to going to school, free of academic pressures.

12. The child's experiences can be manipulated to further his ability to internalize his actions.
13. Preschool experiences increase attentiveness and ability to listen to and follow directions.
14. Children learn to care for themselves and their materials.
15. Preschool education eliminates prejudice and fosters accepting behavior.
16. The program provides a happy place for the child to live with other children and with understanding and helpful teachers.

Criticisms and Difficulties to Be Anticipated — *Do you agree?*

1. Teachers will encounter many disappointments and frustrations.
2. Mothers of young children may be very difficult to work with because of their close attachment to the children, rivalry with the teacher, guilt feelings, and other factors.
3. Children will develop qualities and habits that the parents won't like.
4. The mother may feel that she and the child are growing apart, or that she is being rejected.
5. Very young children need the warmth of the home and the tender love of their mothers.
6. Most preschool programs are baby-sitting operations and pervert the function of the schools.
7. Having the schools take care of infants will make parents even more neglectful than they are.
8. The idea of taking care of people from the cradle to the grave is a communistic concept.
9. Having children in school for years before they settle down to work spoils them for real learning.
10. Qualified teachers and tested programs are not available.
11. Most Head Start teachers do not understand the basic principles of child psychology.
12. Most existing programs are very, very weak.
13. We really do not know how to help very young, disadvantaged children.
14. The initial better adjustment in regular school classes soon fades.
15. Manipulated experiences of school will make children unhappy with their families and homes.

Summary Assessment

A hundred years after Mrs. Carl Schurz opened her home in Watertown, Wisconsin, to the first preschool class in 1855, half the children in America were still without kindergartens. It looks as if preschool education in the years ahead will beat that record. The acute problems of nonmotivated youth in urban communities have caused the federal government to take decisive action. The planning, experimentation, and extension of programs during the past decade have been dramatic.

Many educators have long realized that the formative years of childhood constitute the most vital period of a person's life for shaping attitudes toward himself and others and for planting the seeds of curiosity, initiative, and a desire to succeed. Yet, public junior colleges, technical institutes, colleges, and graduate schools have continued to receive the bulk of attention of educational planners. Ever increasing enrollments at the elementary, secondary, and college levels have exhausted available funds.

The first big thrust for extending education into the earlier years came from the Office of Economic Opportunity and the United States Office of Education. Hand in hand with formal classes for children are nonclassroom experiences, visits to the home, and programs to help parents help their children extend interests and skills. For example, "Sesame Street," a television program designed to develop skills with numbers and letters, has reached perhaps six million children between three and five.

A difference of viewpoint has developed between those who believe in the traditional nursery school approach of warmth, free play, and spontaneous activity and those who advocate structured programs designed to overcome specific deficiencies. The former approach stresses social adjustment, the latter emphasizes academic educability. A common ground must be worked out. Ability to get along with others, emotional stability, and healthy physical development must not be lost sight of in a scramble to increase intellectual capacity to cope with cognitive learning.

A Few Leaders in the Movement

Carl Bereiter	J. McVicker Hunt	Milton J. E. Senn
Benjamin Bloom	James Hymes, Jr.	Evelyn Weber
Martin Deutsch	Lilian G. Katz	David Weikart
Siegfried Engelmann	Katherine Read	Emmy Widmer

A Few Places Where the Innovation Is Used

George Peabody College	Newark, N.J.	Univ. of N. C.
Jackson, Miss.	Shawnee, Okla.	Waterloo, Iowa
Lincoln, Nebr.	Univ. of Chicago	Yale Univ.
Los Angeles, Calif.	Univ. of Ill.	Ypsilanti, Mich.

Bibliography

Bereiter, Carl, "Are Preschool Programs Built the Wrong Way?" *Nation's Schools*, LXXVII, No. 6 (1966), 55-56, 92.

Frymier, Jack R., "Teaching the Young to Love," *The National Elementary Principal*, XLI, No. 2 (1969), 19-21.

Headley, Neith, *The Kindergarten: Its Place in the Program of Education*. New York: The Center for Applied Research in Education, 1965.

Hess, Robert D., and Roberta Meyer Bear, eds., *Early Childhood*. Chicago: Aldine, 1968.

Hickman, L. C., "'Sesame Street' Asks: Can Television Really Teach?" *Nation's Schools*, LXXXV, No. 2 (1970), 58-59.

Katz, Lilian G., "Children and Teachers in Two Types of Head Start Classes," *Young Children*, XXIV, No. 6 (1969), 342-349.

Larrabee, Margery M., "Involving Parents in Their Children's Day-Care Experiences," *Children*, XVI, No. 4 (1969), 149-154.

Read, Katherine H., *The Nursery School*. Philadelphia and London: Saunders, 1966.

Ross, Dorthea and Sheila Ross, "Leniency toward Cheating in Preschool Children," *Journal of Educational Psychology*, LX, No. 6 (1969), 483-487.

Senn, Milton J. E., "Early Childhood Education—For What Goals?" *Children*, XVI, No. 1 (1969), 8-13.

Shuster, Albert H. and Milton E. Ploghoft, *The Emerging Elementary Curriculum*, pp. 169-199. Columbus, Ohio: Merrill, 1970.

Stine, Oscar C., et al., "Selected Neurologic and Behavioral Findings of Children Entering an Early School Admissions Project from Culturally Deprived Neighborhoods," *The Journal of School Health*, XXXIX, No. 7 (1969), 470-477.

Taylor, Katarine Whitside, *Parents and Children Learn Together*. New York: Teachers College, 1969.

Weber, Evelyn, *Early Childhood Education: Perspectives on Change*. Worthington, Ohio: Charles A. Jones, 1970.

Widmer, Emmy Louise, *The Critical Years: Early Childhood Education at the Crossroads*. Scranton, Pa.: International, 1970.

Flexible Scheduling 22

Definition

Flexible scheduling is a procedure by which the school day is so organized as to provide varied lengths of time for different classes and other activities. The term is most commonly applied to schedules in the secondary school. Units of time, usually of 15, 20, 25, or 30 minutes and referred to as *modules,* are used in various multiples. A school employing a 15-minute module, may put two together to constitute a 30-minute period, three to make a 45-minute period, five to build a class period of 75 minutes, or any other combination involving multiples of 15.

Whereas traditional high school schedules employed cycles of one day, repeating the same timetable each day, the typical flexible, or variable, schedule is constructed to repeat itself each week. Some schools have considered a longer cycle. A given class may meet for two long periods and two shorter periods during the week and omit a class session on one of the days or utilize any combination of modules to make up the week's total time allotted for a particular subject.

Flexible scheduling is frequently used with team teaching, in which case the responsibilities of the teachers vary from day to day.

Provision is usually made for large-group presentations, small discussion or inquiry sessions, and individual work. The terms *flexible*, *modular*, and *variable* are usually used interchangeably.

Flexible scheduling should not be looked upon merely as a rearrangement in the time schedule allowing longer periods for one subject than for another, or for more time during the week to be devoted to one course than to another. Basic to it is the effort to improve learning through increased individualization, greater recognition of individual differences, more effective teaching methods, and more adequate provision for developing the student's decision-making and responsibility for organizing his own time and energy.

The amount and arrangement of time is determined by the objectives, activities to be carried out, and facilities available. Planning together, teachers tell the schedule maker the number and varying lengths of the periods, the days and time when the periods should come, and the size of the groups.

Large groups and longer periods are commonly scheduled for showing films, presentations with other visual aids, and testing. Small groups clarify the presentations through discussion, inquiry, and interaction. Independent study allows for enrichment, remediation, and in-depth investigation of individual subjects.

Significant Components *Which are essential?*

1. Before launching on flexible scheduling, administrators and teachers must be sure that they are committed to the idea that learning opportunities are more important than ease of schedule development or convenience of operation.
2. The principal should work with the teachers in developing a flexible schedule since it, more than a traditional schedule, reflects the philosophy of the school and affects the priorities, procedures, and outcomes of instruction.
3. Roles and responsibilities of the principal, teachers, guidance counselors, department heads, team leaders, and others involved should be carefully delineated.
4. Planning time for individuals and teams should be provided.
5. To achieve maximum success, flexible schedule-making should be a year-round activity.
6. Students must understand the reason for flexible scheduling, what opportunities exist for them, and what they must do to make it effective.
7. Grouping and regrouping should be done on the basis of student needs.

8. Involvement of administrators, teachers, students, and the public contributes significantly to acceptance and to hastening the time when the program will operate smoothly and effectively.
9. Those considering flexible scheduling should also consider team teaching.
10. Space is a vital consideration. More space is not always required, but better utilization of space should be effected.
11. An instructional materials center is very important.
12. At the outset of planning, an inventory of space and other facilities should be prepared.
13. Provision should be made to identify and help students who cannot manage open time, and performance criteria should be developed to guide them.
14. Although the goal is to provide a high degree of freedom in planning and using time, the plan must be carefully organized to assure orderly operation.

Proposed Advantages — *With which ones do you agree?*

1. Flexible scheduling moves a big step forward toward individualizing instruction.
2. Flexible scheduling meets the varying time demands of different subjects.
3. A fuller utilization of community resources through study trips that require extended periods of time is made possible.
4. New approaches to learning and innovative ways of teaching are encouraged.
5. Flexible scheduling makes possible more effective and efficient utilization of staff.
6. The variety and challenge which flexible schedules offer sustain interest and decrease boredom.
7. Flexible scheduling allows slow as well as gifted students to proceed at their own rates; they are not paced by rigid class grouping.
8. The opportunity for students to work with teachers on a one-to-one basis is made possible.
9. Teachers conceive of their roles as that of helping students learn rather than that of presenting information.
10. The size of the group can be varied according to the purpose of the instruction, the nature of the content, and the methods to be employed.
11. Flexible scheduling encourages students to experiment with different ways of learning and solving problems.

12. Relief is provided from massive movement of students through the corridors every hour on the hour.
13. More intimate contact with students and their performance enables teachers to assign more reliable grades and makes them more secure about grading.
14. Meetings of department heads, councils, and teaching teams can be scheduled within the regular program.
15. Flexible scheduling makes it easier to expand course offerings.
16. Students are encouraged to assume responsibility for organizing their time and energy.
17. Teachers organize their material better when they are preparing for large-group presentations.

Criticisms and Difficulties to Be Anticipated *Do you agree?*

1. Flexible scheduling requires too much time and effort. Computerizing it is very costly.
2. Varying time allocations will create conflict among teachers who will insist upon more time for their particular subjects.
3. Adequate space and other facilities are not available.
4. If the school becomes involved, it cannot back out if flexible scheduling does not work.
5. A school operating under a flexible schedule falls into confusion and disorder since it is difficult to keep track of students.
6. Teachers may be unwilling or find it impossible to change their methods to make the new program work or may become insecure and frustrated.
7. Because of the many variables involved, teachers will not be able to assign fair grades.
8. Unscheduled periods cause much waste of time as well as behavior problems.
9. Unavoidable cancellation of a field trip, for example, might upset the plan for several weeks.
10. The Carnegie Unit, specifying minimum numbers of periods and minutes per week, presents a real problem; and accrediting agencies, state departments, and colleges are uncooperative.
11. A flexible schedule reduces the teacher's time with students.
12. Some teachers in a team do not do their share.
13. Teachers will experience difficulty in handling the inquiry groups effectively.
14. Students and teachers are likely to be confused.
15. Once the flexible schedule is set, it too becomes rigid; and everybody must adhere to the established plan.

Summary Assessment

In the elementary school, the classroom teacher has, through the years, had a great deal of control over his schedule. In team-teaching programs at the elementary level, teams are relatively free to adapt time to program. However, uniformity and rigidity have characterized traditional schedules in the high school. Each subject is commonly studied for the same length of time each day and for the same number of days and weeks. With few exceptions, the schedule for each day is like that for the other days.

During recent years, recognition of the inadequacy of traditional programs to meet the needs, particularly of alienated youth, has caused educators to search for better structures and methods. Many believe that the practice of instructing high school students as groups is one of the chief roadblocks against individualization. Slowly, but forcefully, the six- or eight-period day is being challenged in urban and rural communities alike. It appears that the number of high schools on some kind of flexible schedule will soon reach 10 per cent of the total. Some adopted flexible schedules, but have reverted to traditional ones because of the confusion that resulted. In some instances, perhaps, this could have been avoided by more thoughtful planning, greater understanding of individualization and commitment to it, and the additional time and work needed to develop conditions essential to success.

There are those who hold that the schedule reveals whether a high school is learning-centered or teaching-centered — whether it exists for students or for the principal and teachers. The computer can be a significant aid to principals who fear that utter confusion will result from making the schedule the servant of the learner. The fact remains, however, that a school can be only as good as its schedule. The philosophical, psychological, and instructional premises that underlie flexible scheduling are, in the main, sound. Arranging time, facilities, and personnel to make it work presents a formidable challenge to those who search for better ways to help students learn.

A Few Leaders in the Movement

David W. Beggs
Lloyd K. Bishop
Frank Brown
Robert Bush
Robert R. Gard
Eugene R. Howard
John Jenkins
Donald Manlove
James Olivero
Theodore R. Storlie
J. Lloyd Trump
W. Deane Wiley

A Few Places Where the Innovation Is Used

Anaheim, Calif.	Livonia, Mich.	North Haven, Conn.
Cohasset, Mass.	Melbourne, Fla.	Poway, Calif.
Flossmoor, Ill.	Montvale, N. J.	Sacramento, Calif.
Holland, Mich.	Newton, Mass.	Skokie, Ill.
Lincoln, Calif.	Norridge, Ill.	Wayland, Mass.

Bibliography

Beggs, David W., III and Edward G. Buffie, *Independent Study — Bold New Ventures.* Bloomington, Ind.: Indiana University, 1965.

Burril, William, "The Modular System at Work," *The Balance Sheet*, L, No. 5 (1969), 214-215, 237.

Bush, Robert N. and Dwight W. Allen, *A New Design for High School Education — Assuming a Flexible Schedule.* New York: McGraw-Hill, 1964.

Doherty, James E., ed., "Are You Afraid of Flexible Scheduling?" *School Management*, XI, No. 5 (1967), 97-102, 104-105, 108.

Gard, Robert R., "A Realistic Look At the Flexible Schedule," *The Clearing House*, XLIV, No. 7 (1970), 425-429.

Hoffman, Orrin, "Flexible Schedule," *Journal of Secondary Education*, XLIII, No. 6 (1968), 278-282.

Leigh, Thomas G., "Big Opportunities in Small Schools Through Flexible — Modular Scheduling," *Journal of Secondary Education*, XLII, No. 4 (1967), 175-187.

Manlove, Donald C. and David W. Beggs, *Flexible Scheduling — Bold New Ventures.* Bloomington, Ind.: Indiana University, 1965.

Petrequin, Gaynor, *Individualizing Learning Through Modular — Flexible Programming.* New York: McGraw-Hill, 1968.

Storlie, Theodore, "Evaluating Flexible Scheduling," *Educational Leadership*, XXV, No. 2 (1967), 177, 179, 181, 183.

Trump, J. Lloyd, "Flexible Scheduling — Fad or Fundamental," *Phi Delta Kappan*, XLIV, No. 8 (1963), 367-371.

Trump, J. Lloyd and Delmas F. Miller, *Secondary Curriculum Improvement*, pp. 307-316. Boston: Allyn and Bacon, 1968.

Wiley, Deane and Lloyd K. Bishop, *The Flexibly Scheduled High School.* New York: Parker, 1968.

Wilmoth, Juanita and Willard Ehn, "The Inflexibility of Flexible Modular Scheduling," *Educational Leadership*, XXVII, No. 7 (1970), 727-731.

Extended School Year 23

Definition

The extended school year is an educational program that offers instruction during the summer on the same basis that it does during the traditional nine months. Frequently it is called the year-round school or the rescheduled school year. Most common among the plans are the rotating term, the year-round acceleration approach, the multiple trails continuous learning program, and the expanded summer school. Both the rotating term plan and the student acceleration approach have several variations in calendar. Chief among these are the quadrimester or quarter system and the trimester system. The quarter plan usually calls for 12-week quarters with a month free in the summer or for four 12-week periods with one week between each. The most common trimester arrangement is that of three periods of 16 weeks with a month off in the summer. The expanded summer school plan provides for a summer program up to eight or nine weeks added to the conventional 180 days.

Pressure for reorganization of the school calendar comes principally from two sources: people stressing economical use of resources and those seeking to extend educational opportunities. Businessmen, school board members, and other economy-minded patrons of the school are sincerely concerned about having expensive school plants idle for a quarter of a year. They see the traditional nine-month program as a stereotype persisting from agrarian days, when young people were needed for work on the farm. Greater use of school plant and fuller utilization of personnel are of genuine concern to them. On the other hand, there are those who believe that the expansion of knowledge and the increased demands of our complex business-industrial life require more and better education for all. They see in the year-round school a possibility for expanding curriculum and reshaping methodology to make them more relevant to changing times and more beneficial to students of varied interests and abilities.

Significant Components *Which are essential?*

1. All those affected must be involved in the planning.
2. Increase in educational opportunity, rather than financial saving, should be the foremost consideration.
3. Valuable experience which students gain from work out of school must not be sacrificed.
4. Time must be allowed for teachers to replenish themselves and their curricula.
5. Programs in the summer must incorporate a broad offering of those activities that can best be carried on during the summer.
6. That plan should be selected which is best suited for a particular community and its existing program.
7. The best plans serve the entire community, are nongraded, and operate for more hours per day and more months per year.
8. The program must provide dynamic curriculum change to gear the schools to the dynamics of societal change.
9. A sound rationale should be worked out for the reasons for the change and for the goals which it seeks.
10. It may be necessary to do away with the Carnegie Unit, specifying minimum minutes of instruction per week; the concept of four years of English or three years of mathematics may have to be discarded.
11. Changes in curriculum such as camping, outdoor education, and work experience are more fundamental and more promising than rearrangements in the calendar.
12. Funds and additional personnel should be provided to plan, explain, make adjustments, and keep the program running smoothly.
13. Effective communication must be established and maintained with the public, students, the board of education, and teachers.
14. An early decision should be made relative to what is mandatory and what is voluntary.
15. Continuous evaluation should be a built-in feature.

Proposed Advantages *With which ones do you agree?*

1. The year-round school provides for greater use of buildings and facilities, fuller utilization of staff, and financial savings.
2. Students can cover more subject matter, accelerate progress, and finish high school at an earlier age.
3. Teachers have an opportunity to earn much-needed money.
4. Children like to be busy in the summer.
5. The need for new plant is reduced by about 20 per cent, and less equipment and fewer books are needed.
6. Greater opportunities are provided for slower learners as well as for the gifted.
7. Delinquency problems, which usually peak in the hot summer when students are out of school, are reduced.
8. Pupils are allowed to enter school at many different times instead of once in a calendar year.
9. Students who are retained do not have to repeat a whole year, and the number of dropouts is decreased.
10. The required number of teachers is reduced, making possible greater teacher selectivity and relieving pressure on the facilities and resources of teacher-education institutions.
11. The extended school year provides a springboard for developing a more flexible curriculum and for introducing innovative practices.
12. Students can get into colleges at different times during the year, as openings become available.
13. Staggered vacations are a convenience to many families since there is a growing tendency on the part of business and industry to set up rotating vacation schedules.
14. The rescheduled school year is particularly beneficial to culturally disadvantaged, physically and mentally handicapped, and emotionally disturbed children.
15. The status and prestige of teachers is enhanced.

Criticisms and Difficulties to Be Anticipated *Do you agree?*

1. The extended school year puts harmful pressure on children.
2. It interferes with vacation plans of parents who do not want their children out of school in the winter.
3. Having several children from one family enrolled in school makes staggered scheduling very difficult.
4. In accelerated programs, students are too young for college or for regular employment when they graduate.

5. Most plans are aimed at saving money, not at increasing benefits for children.
6. The cost of needed air conditioning is substantial, and maintenance and repair become costly in the year-round school.
7. In many states, schools with extended programs run into conflict with statutory requirements.
8. Plans involving rotation can work only in large cities or large districts without causing unduly small classes in some subjects.
9. For many students, necessary sequence in some subjects, such as foreign languages, is broken.
10. Preparing very complex schedules increases work and costs.
11. In many areas summers are too hot for effective study, and winters are too cold for enjoyable vacations.
12. Some students would miss seasonal extracurricular activities.
13. Most teachers want to be free in the summer, and for others the year-round school prevents adequate planning, curriculum development, and continuing education.
14. Under a rotating plan, daytime recreation in the community would have to operate on a year-round basis.
15. During the summer, teachers should work in businesses, laboratories, banks, offices, governmental agencies, or parks learning what they should be teaching in a vital and relevant program.
16. Year-round school programs are apt to emphasize the intellectual to the neglect of the human, beautiful, and functional aspects of life.
17. Attending school all year prevents students from gaining invaluable experience in the outside world, which teaches them to reflect on life, how people become a part of it, and how it becomes a part of them.
18. Young people are young people and need frequent rejuvenation. This nation is wealthy enough to allow them to be just children now and then.
19. Through the years many people have found the long summer months the best part of their school years. Youth should not be made more hostile, angry, and alienated by being required to go to school on a year-round basis.
20. Students will be cut off from camping, scouting, working, loafing, planning their own activities, and other experiences that add significantly to their wholesome maturation.
21. When all factors are considered, the proposed savings disappear rapidly leaving only problems and frustration.

Summary Assessment

Over the years, the basis of interest in the year-round school has shifted significantly. The original advocates of rescheduling stressed the economy resulting from the decrease in classroom demands brought about by acceleration or by rotation of enrollment. Male teachers, particularly, welcomed the possibility of longer employment; but women frequently preferred more vacation time. Administrators appeared to fear additional complexities in scheduling, registering, and staffing. They were also sensitive to adverse reaction of parents who did not want a rotating plan to turn their children out of school in the winter. But gradually educators have begun to recognize the inadequacies of traditional strategies and to see promise in the extended school year.

As positions relative to reorganization of calendars polarized, educators began increasingly to recognize the inadequacies of traditional educational strategies and to sense great potential for curriculum improvement through calendar revision. The extended school year appeared to hold promise for increased flexibility and individualization. Possibilities for program enrichment and provision for handicapped and nonmotivated youth appeared. Advances in the psychology of learning and human adjustment, innovative instructional practices, increase in the quantity and quality of materials, and technological progress all raised hope for changing conventional programs. The growing restlessness of young people raised serious questions about the relevancy and effectiveness of many traditional practices and added urgency to the search for better approaches.

Now when administrators are becoming more willing to give serious consideration to the year-round school, psychologists and curriculum leaders are raising questions. They fear that teachers are too steeped in the traditional stereotype of schooling to launch successfully into a new era of enrichment through individualization. Thoughtful reflection on how the formal and informal educational forces of our times can be integrated for more complete development of youth will enable teachers and their leaders to seize the opportunities and yet avoid the pitfalls of the year-round school.

A Few Leaders in the Movement

Andrew Adams
W. Scott Bauman
David Bjork
Evelyn Carswell
Reid Gillis
George Jensen
Mary Liebman
James Nickerson
Dan Predovich
Clarence Schoenfeldt
George I. Thomas
Herman Torge

A Few Places Where the Innovation Is Used

Ann Arbor, Mich.
Atlanta, Ga.
Enfield, Conn.
Ft. Lauderdale, Fla.
Freeland, Mich.
Hayward, Calif.
Hornell, N.Y.
Langhorne, Pa.
Mankato State College
Port Huron, Mich.
Rochester, Minn.
Romeoville, Ill.
St. Charles, Mo.
Utica, Mich.
Valley View, Ill.

Bibliography

Adams, Andrew, "Look Hard at This Year Round School Plan," *American School Board Journal*, CLVI, No. 1 (1968), 11-15, 31.

Adams, Velma A., "The Extended School Year: A Status Report," *School Management*, XIV, No. 6 (1970), 13-19.

An Appraisal of the Extended School Year. New York: New York State Department of Education Report, 1968.

Childress, Jack R. and Harlan A. Philippi, "Administrative Problems Related to the 11- or 12-month School Year," *The High School Journal*, XLVII, No. 6 (1964), 230-237.

Jensen, George M., "Year-Round School: Can Boards Sidestep It Much Longer?" *American School Board Journal*, CLVII, No. 1 (1969), 8-12.

McLain, John D., *The Flexible All-Year School*. Clarion, Pa.: Research Learning Center, 1969.

The Rescheduled School Year, Research Summary, Research Division — National Education Association. Washington D.C.: National Education Association, 1968.

Scala, Anthony W., "Year-Round School," *Bulletin of the National Association of Secondary School Principals*, LIV, No. 344 (1970), 79-89.

Schoenfeld, Clarence A. and Neil Schmitz, *Year-Round Education*. Madison, Wisc.: Dembar Educational Research Services, 1964.

Setting the Stage for Lengthening School Year Programs, Report for the Governor and the Legislature of the State of New York. Albany, N.Y.: State Education Department, 1968.

Stickler, Hugh and Milton W. Carothers, *The Year-Round Calendar in Operation*. Atlanta, Ga.: Southern Regional Education Board, 1963.

Torge, Herman, "The Year-Round School," Unpublished Master's Thesis, Miami University, Oxford, Ohio, 1968.

West, Paul D. and Douglas G. MacRae, *Fulton County Schools Four Quarter Plan*. Atlanta, Ga.: Fulton County Board of Education, 1969.

Year-Round Education, Mt. Sequoyah National Seminar on Year-Round Education, Fayetteville, Ark.: Arkansas School Study Council, 1969.

Year-Round School, American Association of School Administrators, Library of Congress. Washington, D.C., 1970.

Occupational Education 24

Definition

Occupational education is that aspect of the school program that is directed toward meeting the employment needs of the individual and the manpower demands of society. Programs of various titles and purposes have existed since the early days of the American schools. Trade schools; manual training; continuation schools; mechanics institutes; job training; industrial arts; community colleges; and industrial, vocational, and technical programs have employed various approaches and emphases. Career planning, occupational information, exploration of new fields of interest, consumer education, specialized skills, interpretation of the nature of industrial society, updating and upgrading of competencies, and the safe use of tools and machinery have all received attention.

Occupational education is not new. It is included among the innovative practices of recent years only because of the renewed interest in it on the part of government, education, the general public, business, industry, and the professions. New perspectives, goals, and innovative programs and procedures have been spearheaded by the Vocational Education Act of 1963 and the Vocational Education Amendments of 1968.

The three most common occupational programs of the secondary schools have been industrial arts, vocational education, and technical education. Industrial arts education stresses the need for general education — an understanding of the nature of industry and technology and their relationship to society and the individual. Vocational education emphasizes the development of knowledge, attitudes, interpersonal relations, and specific skills needed for a particular job. Technical education is designed to develop technicians to perform many of the functions formerly carried out by professional personnel.

Among the new approaches stressed by recent legislation, particularly the Vocational Education Amendments of 1968, are cooperative training programs and cooperative work experience programs. Under a carefully developed partnership between the employer and the school, the student in a cooperative training program works with a sponsoring supervisor, a teacher-coordinator, and other teachers at the school in part-time vocational training and part-time employment. Cooperative work experience education is focused on developing positive attitudes, wholesome interests, and good work habits among disadvantaged youth who are alienated from conventional school programs.

Occupational education recognizes that technological changes demand flexibility and new competencies for entry into the first job after school. Orientation to the world of work and experiences with manual, as well as intellectual, effort is essential for helping youth establish their self-identity, develop respect for working people, and assume a constructive role in society. The dignity of work is especially important in our time.

Significant Components *Which are essential?*

1. Programs of occupational training should be relevant and accountable, based on manpower needs, and kept abreast of change in jobs and skill requirements.
2. Vocational programs should provide the options of continuing postsecondary training, taking a job, going to college, or a combination of these.
3. Students should be selected with care, but all students should be selected for something.
4. The student should have a definite career objective, high motivation, and aptitude consistent with his objective.
5. Every effort should be made to prevent vocational programs from becoming dumping grounds for nonmotivated students, or those who cause trouble in academic classrooms.
6. Special provision should be made for the academically and socially disadvantaged and the physically handicapped.

7. Prevocational education for occupational orientation should be provided for children from their initial school experience, and continuing education should extend beyond the regular school years.
8. Councils of business and industrial leaders are necessary for advising and planning, but the educational program should basically rest with educators.
9. The cognitive, affective, and psychomotor proficiency of the student should all receive attention.
10. The purposes and programs of vocational, technical, and work experience for behavioral improvement should be clearly differentiated.
11. In cooperative work education, a competent teacher-coordinator and a positive sponsor are essential.
12. The activities of the work station and the classroom must be carefully integrated.
13. A favorable attitude on the part of labor organizations is desirable.
14. Learning and training, rather than production, should be emphasized.
15. All programs should stress the dignity of work, the worth of people, and the creative aspects of learning.

Proposed Advantages — *With which ones do you agree?*

1. Occupational education develops marketable skills and reduces waste of human resources.
2. Certain subjects such as auto mechanics, typewriting, homemaking, or electricity have great value for personal use and can be correlated with other subjects to provide greater motivation for learning and fuller understanding of the field.
3. Cooperative work education generates support of business and industry for the entire educational program.
4. The program provides an opportunity for youth and their elders to work side by side in a joint enterprise.
5. Occupational education enhances the ability of the consumer to assess and select products of industry intelligently.
6. The satisfaction of getting a job, succeeding, and receiving a paycheck adds zest to a young person's life.
7. By providing opportunities for success, occupational education builds self-assurance in many who do not excel in academic areas.

8. Through face-to-face encounters and close supervision of work, opportunity is provided for individualization of instruction, guidance, and counseling.
9. Occupational education effectively builds responsibility.
10. There is added respect for work and the working man.
11. Particularly to disadvantaged youth, achievement in vocational and technical work is real and significant.
12. Business and industry provide relevant, costly laboratories that would otherwise be unavailable for instruction.
13. Occupational education offers opportunity for creative expression and enhances ability in solving problems.
14. The value of proficiency and excellence is more convincingly demonstrated than in many other subject fields.
15. Cooperative work education makes schools aware of changes and stimulates them to keep the curriculum up to date.
16. Occupational education offers hope for coping with problems of disadvantaged youth by helping them become contributing members of society.

Criticisms and Difficulties to Be Anticipated — *Do you agree?*

1. Industry does not understand the problems of schools or the purposes of their programs, and schools do not understand the needs and programs of industry and business.
2. Overprotective social taboos and legal obstacles stand in the way of providing significant work experience at an early age, when it would be a genuinely valuable learning opportunity.
3. Restrictive educational requirements of state departments, colleges, and local schools obstruct progress.
4. Many teachers seem to believe that real learning cannot take place unless the student is sitting at a desk with a book listening to the teacher.
5. One of the distinct difficulties in cooperative work experience is that of preventing the urge for performance and production from overshadowing learning and the learner.
6. The mobility of our population and the danger of obsolescence make preparation for specific jobs unrealistic.
7. Vocational education neglects social, intellectual, and emotional development.
8. Occupational education contents itself with isolated bits of knowledge and routine skills to the neglect of concepts, generalizations, and principles.
9. Many of the facilities needed for adequate vocational-technical education are excessively costly.

10. Lack of desire, initiative, and responsibility, rather than of specific skills, are the ingredients of unemployability.
11. Defensiveness and insecurity of public school teachers, including industrial arts teachers, are a real obstacle to imaginative programs of occupational education.
12. Cooperative work education focuses attention on earning rather than on learning.
13. Occupational programs will be the dumping ground for non-motivated students and behavior problems.
14. Most businesses and industries will not make the commitment necessary for effective occupational education.

Summary Assessment

The problems that face people shape the direction of their energy and efforts as a society and as individuals. At times these demands are long-term, at others they are focused on temporary emergencies. From the time of the Pilgrims through the years of the frontier, physical survival was the most urgent problem. Production of food, clothing and shelter required top priority in the job market. The advent of electricity, the railroad, the telephone, the automobile, and the farm tractor caused occupational changes in their time similar to those occasioned by the introduction of the computer. Time and human energy were released to refocus on new ventures.

The occupational requirements of the years ahead likewise will be determined by the kind of society that evolves and by the priorities that it establishes. Accelerated change will quicken the demand for new competencies and for their continuous upgrading. The idea that occupational education equips the young for occupations and professions will rapidly disappear as schools realize that they can prepare youth only for entry into an occupation. Technological sophistication, social complexities, and an ever accelerating rate of change demand education from the cradle to the grave. Preservice, inservice, and postservice education will all assume greater significance. How much of it is to be provided by private enterprise and by public agencies is yet to be determined.

Education for a technological age must not neglect the affective areas of learning if man is to retain mastery of the machine and control of his own destiny. Only through combining careful study of values with vocational-technical skills can society give desirable direction to scientific and technological change.

A Few Leaders in the Movement

Melvin L. Barlow	Lowell A. Burkett	Silvius G. Harold
John A. Beaumont	Leslie H. Cochran	H. H. London
George L. Brandon	Rupert N. Evans	Carl J. Schaefer

A Few Places Where the Innovation Is Used

Bucks County, Pa.	Fort Wayne, Ind.	Penta-County Voc. School and Tech. Coll.
Cleveland, Ohio	Miami-Dade Jr. Coll.	Stout State Univ.
Dayton, Ohio	Milwaukee Tech. Coll.	Univ. of Minn.
Detroit, Mich.	New York, N.Y.	

Bibliography

Barlow, Melvin L., *History of Industrial Education in the United States.* Peoria, Ill.: Charles A. Bennett, 1967.

Burkett, Lowell A., ed., "Research Visibility," *American Vocational Journal,* XLIV, No. 4 (1969), 33-48.

———, ed., "Research Visibility," *American Vocational Journal,* XLIV, No. 7 (1969), 33-48.

———, ed., "Research Visibility," *American Vocational Journal,* XLV, No. 1 (1970), 45-60.

Burt, Samuel M., *Industry and Vocational-Technical Education.* New York: McGraw-Hill, 1967.

Cochran, Leslie H., *Innovative Programs in Industrial Education.* Bloomington, Ill.: McKnight, 1970.

Evans, Rupert N., "Advantages, Disadvantages, and Factors in Development," *American Vocational Journal,* XLIV, No. 5 (1969), 19-22, 58.

Giachino, J. W. and Ralph O. Gallington, *Course Construction in Industrial Arts, Vocational and Technical Education.* Chicago: American Technical Society, 1968.

Huffman, Harry, "Cooperative Vocational Education," *American Vocational Journal,* XLIV, No. 5 (1969), 16-18.

Reed, Donald R., "The Nature and Function of Continuation Education," *Journal of Secondary Education,* XLIV, No. 7 (1969), 292-297.

Ryan, Charles W., "Innovations in Career Development," *Vocational Education,* XLIV, No. 3 (1969), 63-65.

Schaffer, George M., "Gearing the Area Vo-Tech School for Service in the 70's," *School Shop,* XXIX, No. 8 (1970), 126-130.

Teeple, John B., "Planning Vocational Programs to Meet National Goals," *American Vocational Journal,* XLIV, No. 8 (1969), 31-33.

Trump, J. Lloyd and Delmas F. Miller, *Secondary Curriculum Improvement,* pp. 208-222. Boston: Allyn and Bacon, 1968.

Part Five
Personnel Utilization and Improvement

Collective Negotiations 25

Definition

In the context of public education, collective negotiations are formalized procedures by which one or more representatives of a teacher group and of a board of education attempt to work out an agreement setting forth the terms and conditions of employment for teachers and of other matters that have been determined by the two parties. Although boards often negotiate with other groups of employees, the present discussion is limited to negotiations with certified personnel.

The process includes identifying concerns, resolving differences, arriving at a mutually-acceptable position, and writing a master contract that will govern the operations of a school district for a specified period of time. Contracts usually contain grievance procedures for resolving disputes over alleged violation of contracts.

In case of an impasse, negotiation agreements often provide for mediation, fact-finding, and arbitration. The mediator tries to achieve agreement through persuasion, suggestion, and advice. The fact-finder reviews data relating to the impasse and makes a report and recommendations for resolving differences. His recommendations may be accepted or rejected by the negotiators. Similarly, the arbitrator considers the differences and makes decisions resolving them; but they are usually binding.

"Good faith" bargaining is basic to collective negotiations. It is commonly accepted to mean that the negotiators refrain from making irresponsible proposals, seriously consider the proposals of both parties, and reject none without good reason. Most commonly negotiated issues are differences relating to salary schedules, extra pay, calendar, grievance procedures, work load, released time, class size, fringe benefits, no strike provisions, and nonprofessional duties.

There is little substantive difference between the terms *collective bargaining*, *collective negotiations*, and *professional negotiations*. Similarly, it is difficult to identify differences between the approaches of so-called professional organizations and of teacher unions. The most common pattern of development finds teacher organizations actively promoting compulsory negotiations and boards opposing them.

Much of the early legislation relating to collective negotiations was developed in Connecticut during the 1950's. After 1960, Connecticut, Massachusetts, Michigan, New Jersey, New York, and other states enacted legislation requiring boards of education to bargain with certificated personnel. The statutes of many states still prohibit boards from entering into formal agreements for collective bargaining.

The rapid spread of negotiation procedures is furthered by some extreme and selfish positions of militant teachers and by some cases of authoritarian indifference of boards and administrators toward the legitimate concerns of their employees.

Significant Components — *Which are essential?*

1. The negotiating instrument must set forth well-defined conditions and procedures for initiating and conducting negotiations.
2. One bargaining unit should be determined.
3. Before negotiating, there should be agreement on the items to be negotiated; new ones should not be introduced later.
4. Patience and willingness to devote the time necessary to reach mutually acceptable solutions are essential.
5. In most instances it is not considered good practice for board members to be part of the negotiating team.
6. The superintendent should be the chief advisor to the management team.
7. Items of minor disagreement should be considered first, and major differences left until last.
8. Both parties must feel accountable for the results.

9. Supervisory personnel should be placed on the negotiating team only after careful deliberation.
10. Provisions must be made for impasse and should be clearly understood by both parties.
11. It must be recognized that flexibility and responsiveness are not the same as capitulation. Good faith on the part of both parties is essential.
12. Teacher-representatives should be assured freedom from reprisals.
13. Honesty, frankness, and common sense should govern the actions of both parties.
14. To avoid having agreements rejected, negotiation teams must remain in close contact with their constituencies.
15. Outbursts of temper, hostility, threats, inflamatory language, and personality conflicts should be avoided.
16. Respect for the integrity, responsibility, and prerogatives of teachers and board members must prevail.

Proposed Advantages *With which ones do you agree?*

1. Improving conditions of employment creates an improved educational climate and enhances opportunities for children.
2. Failure to negotiate causes greater division between management and employees than actual negotiations do.
3. Teachers are professional people, who should have reasonable autonomy and participate in decision-making.
4. Keeping salaries and other benefits abreast of those of other professional groups makes teachers more willing to accept increased hours of work, growing demands for additional training, and expanding problems of teaching more difficult children.
5. Negotiations provide a safety valve for preventing sanctions, strikes, and other work stoppages.
6. Sharing decision-making, although commonly resisted by management, is much better than the loss of morale resulting from unilateral decisions.
7. Negotiations enable the teachers and boards to bring their concerns out into the open.
8. Teachers need an outlet for consideration of constructive suggestions that are otherwise ignored.
9. Collective negotiation agreements establish orderly procedures for resolving conflicts and provide stability and continuity of operation during periods of unrest.
10. Festering irritations that detract from effective performance are eliminated.

11. Negotiations develop broader perspective and greater responsibility among employees and employers.
12. Negotiations are a springboard for improving teacher performance.
13. Participation in decision-making enables teachers to police their own ranks and to improve professional standards.

Criticisms and Difficulties to Be Anticipated *Do you agree?*

1. Negotiations and grievance procedures generate a search for dissatisfactions where none would otherwise emerge.
2. The sudden demand for collective negotiations has sprung from the rivalry between the American Federation of Teachers (AFT) and the National Education Association (NEA).
3. The public views collective bargaining, sanctions, and strikes as activities unbecoming a professional teacher.
4. Teacher militancy generates unrest among students and deterioration in discipline.
5. Public employees should not be allowed to engage in collective bargaining or work stoppages.
6. Negotiations often lead to increased costs and less service.
7. Invariably, the need for more supplies, maintenance, and equipment is neglected by pressure to divert money to teacher benefits.
8. The labor-management model does not fit professionals.
9. Tensions and conflicts are increased because negotiations assume that the parties are antagonists, and ugly scars remain after negotiations are completed.
10. Contracts violate the principle of individual differences and individualization of treatment.
11. Negotiations alienate taxpayers.
12. Continuous wrangling and confrontation consume too much energy and detract significantly from the joy and satisfaction of teaching.
13. A definite conflict of interest exists when teachers establish priorities for the allocation of public funds.
14. Boards of education do not understand the feelings, commitment, and concerns of teachers; and teachers do not appreciate the responsibility, pressures, and limitations of the board.
15. Collective negotiations destroy administrative authority and leave nobody responsible to the public.
16. Frequently, both parties make unrealistic demands.

17. Often association leaders do not present the views of their membership, and boards do not represent the citizens.
18. Dedicated teachers are intimidated by militant leaders.
19. Spelling out in detail duties, uniform class size, and time commitments discourages experimentation and innovation.
20. Negotiations merely provide a platform for malcontents.
21. The welfare of children is not negotiable.
22. Teaching is different from other professions since it is supported by public funds and virtually has a monopoly.

Summary Assessment

The spread of collective negotiations has been one of the most dramatic, controversial, and perhaps fundamental educational developments of recent years. Many educators as well as lay citizens are deeply disturbed by the movement. Others view it as a breakthrough for long overdue educational reform.

Although the proponents insist that collective negotiations are designed to establish an orderly means of resolving differences and providing stability through contractual agreement, negotiations often develop into a bitter power struggle.

Insistence upon rights, sometimes with disregard for commensurate responsibilities, has sharpened differences among all groups in our social structure. In education, the competition between the NEA and the AFT for achieving economic concessions for their members, sanctions, and teacher strikes have confounded boards and administrators and bewildered pupils and parents. Arbitrary and unreasonable boards, few as they may be, too often have been insensitive to sincere and legitimate requests of teachers. They have contributed to the pressure for collective negotiations. Competing teacher organizations probably will move in the direction of mergers. Negotiations will become more sophisticated and responsible. As educators and the public demand greater state support for schools, it is probable that teachers will turn more and more to the states to negotiate their requests, and that harassed and weary boards will welcome such a turn.

Public demand for accountability is likely to shift the emphasis from considerations of work load and economic welfare to provisions that will give specific promise for improved performance and productivity. Working together as equals, boards, administrators, and teachers must jointly develop policies to improve the quality of education and see to it that their policies work.

If properly directed and skillfully executed, collective negotiations add excitement and satisfaction to all those involved in education. It appears that negotiations are here to stay. Whether they are a boon or a plague rests with all those involved.

A Few Leaders in the Field

Luvern Cunningham	Myron Lieberman	George W. Taylor
Stanley Elam	Michael Moskow	Wesley A. Wildman
John H. Fisher	Charles R. Perry	David H. Wollett

Bibliography

Bowers, Raymond W., ed., *Studies on Behavior in Organizations*, pp. 101-134, Athens, Ga.: University of Georgia, 1966.

Carlton, Patrick W. and Harold I. Goodwin, eds., *The Collective Dilemma: Negotiations In Education*. Worthington, Ohio: Charles A. Jones, 1969.

Elam, Stanley, Myron Lieberman, and Michael H. Moskow, *Collective Negotiations in Public Education*. Chicago: Rand McNally, 1967.

Elkin, Sol M., "Another Look at Collective Negotiations," *School and Society*, XCVIII, No. 2324 (1970), 173-175.

Heald, James E. and Samuel A. Moore, II, *The Teacher and Administrative Relationships in School Systems*, pp. 247-263. New York: Macmillan, 1968.

Law, Kenneth L., "The Real Heart of a Negotiated Agreement," *Today's Education*, LXIX, No. 2 (1970), 36-38.

Lieberman, Myron, "Get Ready to Negotiate with Nonteaching Employees," *School Management*, LIII, No. 11 (1969), 32-38.

———, "Negotiating with Teachers," *School Management*, XIII, No. 3 (1969), 38-40, 42, 44.

Lieberman, Myron and Michael H. Moskow, *Collective Negotiations for Teachers: An Approach to School Administration*. Chicago: Rand McNally, 1966.

Perry, Charles R. and Wesley A. Wildman, *The Impact of Negotiations in Public Education: The Evidence from the Schools*. Worthington, Ohio: Charles A. Jones, 1970.

Shannon, Thomas A., "The Principal's Management Role in Collective Negotiations, Grievances and Strikes," *Journal of Secondary Education*, XLV, No. 2 (1970), 51-56.

Stinnett, T. M., Jack H. Kleinmann, and Martha L. Ware, *Professional Negotiations in Public Education*. New York: Macmillan, 1966.

Taylor, George W., "The Public Interest in Collective Negotiations in Education," *Phi Delta Kappan*, XLVIII, No. 1 (1966), 16-22.

Weinstock, Henry R. and Paul L. Van Horn, "Impact of Negotiations Upon Public Education," *The Clearing House*, XLIII, No. 6 (1969), 358-363.

Differentiated Staffing 26

Definition

Differentiated staffing is a plan providing for differentiated student needs, interests, and abilities through more effective deployment and utilization of differentiated teacher interests, talents, ambitions, and skills. Basically, it is a process of matching teaching with learning and of eliminating inefficiency resulting from mismatches. It is based on the premise that redeployment of teaching personnel and more effective use of special talents will provide greater opportunity for individualization of instruction and clinical teaching. The learning experiences of pupils are likely to be enriched, and teachers and paraprofessionals can benefit from the interaction within the team.

Inherent in the program is increased professional autonomy and involvement of professional personnel in planning and decision-making. Subprofessionals perform technical, clerical, and routine functions, thus making the varied competencies of professionals available for higher-level instructional responsibilities.

Concentrated study of more effective utilization of teaching personnel was begun by J. Lloyd Trump in the early 1960's. Such men as Dwight Allen developed paper models, converted them to operational plans, and subjected them to practical application. Temple City, California, was perhaps the earliest system to test a hierarchical model of differentiated staffing. The program includes four levels of teachers: master teachers, senior teachers, staff teachers, and associate teachers. Teacher aides, resource center assistants, and laboratory assistants are included among the subprofessionals. Beaverton, Oregon, and several county systems in Florida are representative of other schools that have given intensive study to staff deployment and utilization. Another plan of staff organization, known as synergetic or cooperative team teaching, considers all qualified teachers as equals.

Significant Components — *Which are essential?*

1. Learning needs of students should determine the organizational plan for staffing; and better instruction, rather than economy, must be its goal.
2. Ideally, the plan should be initiated by the teachers, and they must have leadership roles in developing the model.
3. Community understanding and support must be developed.
4. Flexible scheduling is indispensable for utilization of various staff talents.
5. Those concerned must feel that the staffing plan is fair and can be justified by its contribution to learning.
6. Objective and detailed job descriptions are essential.
7. Greater autonomy must be given to the staff of a school.
8. Flexible space and a good learning center are necessary.
9. Adequate time must be provided for group planning.
10. Administrators must be willing to become partners with teachers in decision-making.
11. To expect promotions and salaries above those of their colleagues, teachers must understand what leadership and additional responsibility on their part mean.
12. All members of the hierarchy should teach for at least part of the day.
13. The higher levels of the hierarchy must be seen as positions of service rather than of authority.

Proposed Advantages — *With which ones do you agree?*

1. Differentiated staffing increases the opportunity for greater individualization of instruction and more diversified and beneficial group activities.

2. Pupils have contact with a variety of talents and skills.
3. Differentiated staffing enables competent personnel whose first love is teaching to attain prestige, satisfaction, and financial reward without leaving the classroom to go into administration.
4. Accompanying new authority and decision-making will be new responsibility on the part of teachers.
5. Beginning teachers are placed in continuous contact with leaders of outstanding ability and given the opportunity to work into the profession gradually.
6. Associate and staff teachers are relieved of the insecurity and anxiety resulting from having to carry responsibilities they feel they are not qualified to discharge.
7. The plan makes teaching a profession by giving practitioners a part in establishing standards, determining direction and goals, and enjoying career incentives.
8. Teachers are given a choice in the roles they feel best qualified to play, the responsibilities they want to assume, and the number of months they want to work.
9. Differentiation of roles throws out the traditional false assumption that all teachers are equal.
10. Differentiated staffing helps to bridge the widening gap between teachers and administrators.
11. The plan will reshape graduate teacher education by emphasizing better instruction rather than courses in law, finance, public relations, buildings, and business procedures often pursued by teachers who, for financial reasons, aspire to administrative positions, but continue in the classroom for their entire careers.
12. Undergraduate students will direct their efforts toward developing competence rather than toward passing courses required for certification.
13. Subprofessionals relieve teachers of routine functions and free them for creative work with children.
14. Peer evaluation for promotion generates confidence in the system and promotes professional responsibility.
15. Unity of purpose and teamwork are stimulated.
16. Provision is made for meeting the need for specialization required by the rapid expansion of knowledge, sophisticated technological development, and improvement in teaching strategies and techniques.
17. Differentiated staffing provides a basis for salary differentiation which teachers, administrators, and board members can accept.

Criticisms and Difficulties to Be Anticipated *Do you agree?*

1. At present there is no valid way of deciding the comparative value of different tasks in the totality of teaching.
2. Although the hierarchical model proposes to produce teamwork, it will in reality have a splintering effect.
3. The plan is a surreptitious way of putting in a merit pay plan and exploiting teachers.
4. To put a plan of differentiated staffing into operation, many of the salaries of associate and staff teachers will have to be cut; and they will leave.
5. The plan will lower the prestige and self-image of all teachers except the master.
6. The competent teacher is not necessarily the competent coordinator of the efforts of others, the perceptive developer of curriculum, or the skillful supervisor.
7. Teachers, who have always considered themselves coequals, resent the idea of a hierarchy.
8. By fostering specialization, the system moves the school away from being child-centered to being subject-centered.
9. Many of the most competent prospective leaders do not want to work on a twelve-month schedule.
10. Parents will want to deal only with the master teacher.
11. Teachers want the additional salary and prestige, but will still expect administrators to carry the responsibility.
12. If strong leaders emerge among the teachers, insecure administrators will resent them.
13. Seniority and college degrees should have no relationship to the hierarchy except as they influence demonstrable competence in leadership.
14. Often the staff teacher will actually be more competent than the master teacher and will resent the differentiation in roles and salary.
15. Differentiation is a plan designed to help administrators weed out some teachers and advance their favorites.
16. Differentiated staffing would be unnecessary if principals would stop tinkering with managerial routine and become meaningfully involved in teaching and learning.
17. If the higher level personnel are not on tenure, they will be at the mercy of those lower in the echelon; and the majority of teaching positions will be cozy places for those who have little ambition.

Summary Assessment

Although the idea of differentiated staffing is relatively new, the interest that it has generated indicates that it will receive continued attention. Occasional reference is still made to reduced costs, but the mainstream of current thinking is directed toward improvement of learning through better planning and better utilization of talent. In fact, it is quite generally agreed that, except where unusual volunteer resources are available, costs will not be reduced.

The program is more than a redeployment of teaching personnel. It constitutes a basic change in philosophy relative to what teaching and learning are. The structure of school organization, planning, and decision-making is intricately involved. It is commonly agreed that there is a place for both administrators and instructional leaders. How their roles can complement one another to achieve more effectively the purpose of the schools needs intensive study and analysis.

For example, "supervision" of study halls, cafeterias, and corridors is usually among the first duties assigned to paraprofessionals. Here only superprofessionals can really teach proper attitudes, values, respect for one another, responsibility, and orderly conduct. Special talent and deep insights are required. Here paraprofessionals cannot teach; they can only patrol.

As one reflects on the proposed advantages of differentiated staffing and its criticisms, problems, and pitfalls, he is struck by the great number of arguments that can be presented both for and against it. One of the more baffling problems is that of determining the different levels of responsibility, assigning duties to the respective levels, and assessing the competencies required. Many teachers fear that the plan is a scheme to exploit them. Conservative administrators are reluctant to involve teachers in policy development and decision-making. Others see better staff utilization as another significant move toward providing an education appropriate to each child. The advocates of the plan insist that it will put teaching on the broad, though bumpy, road to becoming a true profession.

A Few Leaders in the Movement

Dwight Allen	Robert Gourley	Donald M. Sharpe
Lloyd K. Bishop	Myron Lieberman	Rodney P. Smith
Roy E. Edelfelt	Bernard McKenna	Joseph Stocker
Fenwick English	M. John Rand	J. Lloyd Trump

A Few Places Where the Innovation Is Used

Beaverton, Oreg.	Fountain Valley, Calif.	Sarasota, Fla.
Cherry Creek, Colo.	Greenwich, Conn.	Temple City, Calif.
Claremont, Calif.	Kansas City, Mo.	Warren, Ohio
Dade County, Fla.	Mankato State College	Williamsville, N.Y.

Bibliography

Differentiated Staffing in Schools, Education U. S. A. Special Report, Washington, D. C.: National School Public Relations Association, 1970.

Edelfelt, Roy A., "Differentiated Staffing: Is It Worth the Risk?" *New York State Education*, LVII, No. 6 (1970), 22-24.

English, Fenwick, "The Differentiated Staff: Education's Technostructure," *Educational Technology*, X, No. 2 (1970), 24-27.

———, "Teacher May I? Take Three Giant Steps! The Differentiated Staff," *Phi Delta Kappan*, LI, No. 4 (1969), 211-214.

Hickman, L. C., ed., "Differentiated Staffing," *Nation's Schools*, LXXXV, No. 6 (1970), 43-49.

Joyce, Bruce R., "Staff Utilization," *Review of Educational Research*, XXXVII, No. 3 (1967), 323-336.

Krumbein, Gerald, "How to Tell Exactly What Differentiated Staffing Will Cost Your District," *The American School Board Journal*, CLVII, No. 11 (1970), 19-24.

McKenna, Bernard H., *Staffing the Schools*. New York: Bureau of Publications, Teachers College, Columbia, 1965.

Olivero, James L. and Edward G. Buffie, eds., *Educational Manpower: From Aids to Differentiated Staff Patterns*. Bloomington, Ind.: Indiana University, 1970.

Rand, M. John, "Case for Differentiated Staffing," *Journal California Teachers Association*, LXV, No. 2 (1969), 29-33.

Rand, M. John and Fenwick English, "Towards a Differentiated Teaching Staff," *Phi Delta Kappan*, XLIX, No. 5 (1968), 264-268.

Stocker, Joseph, *Differentiated Staffing in Schools*. Washington: National School Public Relations Association, 1970.

Teacher Education Issues and Innovations. The American Association of Colleges for Teacher Education Yearbook, Washington, D.C., 1968, 78-104.

Trump, J. Lloyd, *Images of the Future*. Commission on the Experimental Study of the Utilization of the Staff in the Secondary School. Library of Congress, Washington, D. C., 1959, 13-14.

Team Teaching 27

Definition

Team teaching is a process involving two or more teachers who work together closely in planning, carrying out, and evaluating the learning experiences of a group of students usually the size of two to four conventional classes. The students may work as one large group, in small groups, or as individuals. Team teaching is more than an organizational pattern developed to make efficient use of staff, space, and equipment. Basically it is a philosophy of learning designed to vitalize the curriculum, develop more confident and competent teachers, and individualize instruction.

Some teams are made up of teachers from the same or closely related fields who work on a vertical basis with students in all grades. Other teams are composed of several teachers who work on a horizontal level with students of the same grade or a limited number of grades. In addition to certified teachers with special competence in various aspects of the instructional program, most teams include clerical aides, technical assistants, and other paraprofessionals.

The keys to success are cooperation, preplanning, flexibility in scheduling, variety of materials, and individualization. Pooling the professional and personal strengths of each of the team members offers richer opportunities to the pupils and stimulates professional growth of the teachers. Essential for smooth and effective operation is a team leader knowledgeable in curriculum development with special skill in group dynamics. Begun at the high school level, team teaching is currently popular in middle schools and is gaining acceptance at the elementary level, particularly in nongraded programs.

Significant Components *Which are essential?*

1. Before launching on a team teaching program, the staff should engage in extensive planning and visit other schools.
2. The teachers must be committed to working as a team, sensitive to one another's views, and ready for new roles.
3. The leader should possess strong leadership qualities, sound knowledge, and skill in curriculum development.
4. Supporting personnel, clerical and technical, are needed to free regular teachers from routine duties.
5. Space and materials for large and small group instruction and for individual study are necessary.
6. Every member of the team should be involved in the planning from the beginning and should have regular time for continuous planning.
7. Schedules with maximum flexibility add to success.
8. The teachers should complement one another in temperament, background, interests, and special talents.
9. Effective communication is needed within the team and with all other segments of the school.
10. Provision for independent study, experimentation, and a wide range of projects and activities is invaluable.
11. Administrators, particularly building principals, must understand the purposes and processes and participate actively.
12. Orientation and provision for continuing inservice development is needed, particularly for inexperienced teachers.
13. Students must be prepared for team teaching.
14. Evaluation should include not only pupil learning, but also the assessment of the team operation, with emphasis on intragroup relations.
15. It is usually better to move into team teaching on a limited basis than to try to reorganize the entire school at one time.

Proposed Advantages *With which ones do you agree?*

1. Team teaching provides an opportunity to utilize the strengths and discard the weaknesses of both the self-contained and departmentalized programs.
2. The difference in personalities of team members enables each child to find one teacher with whom he relates exceptionally well.

3. Presentation, followed by student-led discussion groups, develops leadership and improves communication skills.
4. Team teaching provides a laboratory for planning and testing other innovations.
5. Special teachers can be meaningfully involved in an integrated learning program.
6. Working together develops teamwork in the staff.
7. Flexible schedules and provision for one-to-one instruction contribute to individualization.
8. As a partner and a guide at the same time, the team leader is in a strategic position to help inexperienced members of the team in their professional growth.
9. Better objectives, instructional procedures, and evaluation can be effected by pooling thinking.
10. Members of the team receive professional stimulation from observing their colleagues, being observed, and sharing their own successes with others.
11. Independent study promotes self-reliance in the students.
12. The program allows for better utilization of personnel, space, material, and equipment.
13. The large group provides opportunity for identifying students of complementary interests and talents who can work together to their mutual advantage.
14. Cooperative planning, so extensively used in the teams, is vital to effective curriculum revision and improvement.
15. Team teaching and nongraded programs support and complement each other.
16. Availability of clerical and technical assistants allows the teacher to devote his time to professional duties.
17. Teachers and students are more enthusiastic.

Criticisms and Difficulties to Be Anticipated — *Do you agree?*

1. Effective team teachers are hard to find; few colleges are turning them out.
2. Competent team leaders are extremely scarce.
3. Some competent teachers prefer to work alone.
4. In the elementary school, team teaching tends to destroy the values of the self-contained classroom by introducing excessive departmentalization.
5. Some students and teachers experience difficulty in adjusting to large groups or to flexible schedules.
6. Failure to provide orientation, preparation, and planning time will render the effort ineffective.

7. Unless guarded against, rivalry and strife may spring up within the team.
8. In a team situation, it may be difficult to allocate responsibility to one teacher for lack of achievement or undesirable conduct on the part of an individual student.
9. Only through effective communication can public misunderstanding be averted.
10. Failure to provide adequate facilities could be an insurmountable obstacle.
11. Some administrators think that nothing can be done by a team that could not be done by a good teacher.
12. Teachers who are not imbued with the philosophy of team teaching may quickly pervert it to "turn" teaching, allowing some to waste time while others carry the full responsibility.
13. Unwillingness of some members of the team to do their share is likely to cause friction.
14. Lack of rigid structure may appear to be disorder.
15. Increase in salary and other costs will result.
16. Students will pit one teacher against another.
17. Prima donnas, no matter how competent, will ruin the team.

Summary Assessment

There is little disagreement with the philosophy, purpose, and even most of the proposed advantages of team teaching. More argument arises over the possibilities for its successful implementation. Few of the objections or reservations expressed are insurmountable, but several of them—including lack of committed teachers, adequate space, and necessary facilities—should receive serious consideration.

The chief value of team teaching lies in its potentialities for enabling students to pursue learning activities appropriate to their needs and learning styles. Large group experiences, discussion groups, and independent study provide varied advantages. The careful planning and cooperative effort demonstrated in a good team teaching situation can encourage teamwork and improve morale among teachers and students. Independent study should foster self-reliance and responsibility.

More important than the obstacles commonly cited, perhaps, is the unwillingness of many educators to cut loose from their traditional moorings. In order to approach its promise and potential, team teaching must be grounded upon a philosophy of creativity, teamwork, thoughtful planning, flexibility, and individualization. Those who hold with rigid standards, neat organization, and conformity find little comfort or challenge in teaming. Even more disturbing to them may be the realization that team teaching, more than most innovations, provides a seedbed for other changes. Yet, the enthusiasm generated by having groups of teachers thinking, planning, and working together might easily set off chain reactions that could lead far beyond the bounds of traditional thinking.

A Few Leaders in the Movement

Robert H. Anderson
Medill Bair
Ethel Bears
David Beggs
Robert W. Jones
Henry F. Olds
Judson T. Shaplin
Harold Spears
J. Lloyd Trump

A Few Places Where the Innovation Is Used

Auburn, Maine
Carmel, Calif.
El Dorado, Ark.
Evanston, Ill.
Fort Wayne, Ind.
High Springs, Fla.
Lexington, Mass.
Melbourne, Fla.
Norwalk, Conn.
Plainview, N.Y.
Racine, Wis.
Univ. of Wis.

Bibliography

Anderson, Robert H., *Teaching in a World of Change*, pp. 71-108. New York: Harcourt, 1966.

Beggs, David W., ed., *Team Teaching: Bold New Venture*. Bloomington, Ind.: Indiana University, 1964.

Bair, Medill and Richard G. Woodward, *Team Teaching in Action*. Boston: Houghton Mifflin, 1964.

Davis, Harold S. and Ellsworth Tompkins, *How To Organize an Effective Team Teaching Program*. Englewood Cliffs, N.J.: Prentice-Hall, 1966.

Hanslousky, Glenda, Sue Moyer, and Helen Wagner, *Why Team Teaching?* Columbus, Ohio: Merrill, 1969.

Inlow, Gail M., *The Emergent In Curriculum*, pp. 287-306. New York: Wiley, 1966.

Oliva, Peter F., *The Secondary School Today*. Scranton, Pa.: International, 1968.

Peterson, Carl H., *Effective Team Teaching: The Easton Area High School Programs*. West Nyack, N.Y.: Parker, 1966.

Polos, Nicholas C., *The Dynamics of Team Teaching*. Dubuque, Iowa: William C. Brown, 1965.

Shaplin, Judson and Henry F. Olds, *Team Teaching*. New York: Harper, 1964.

Shawver, David E., "Team Teaching: How Successful Is It?" *The Clearing House*, XLIII, No. 1 (1968), 21-26.

Wey, Herbert W., *Handbook for Principals*, pp. 35-38. New York: Schaum, 1966.

Courtesy Albuquerque, New Mexico, Public Schools

Up! up! my friend, and quit your books;
Or surely you'll grow double:
Up! up! my friend, and clear your looks;
Why all this toil and trouble?

One impulse from a vernal wood
May teach you more of man,
Of moral evil and of good,
Than all the sages can.

Wordsworth

Teacher Aides

28

Definition

Except for rare instances, the terms *teacher aides, paraprofessionals, auxiliary school personnel, teacher assistants, nonprofessionals,* and *subprofessionals* are used interchangeably. They are volunteers or paid employees of the school who relieve the teacher of nonprofessional duties thus freeing him for the professional responsibilities of teaching. The duties of aides vary according to the demands of the individual school and the qualifications of the aide. However, a distinction is generally made between the instructional and noninstructional duties. Assisting the teacher with large-group instruction, working with small groups or individual pupils, reading stories, dictating spelling words, and helping a student who has been absent from school are referred to as "instructional duties." Among the "noninstructional services" are clerical work, counting money, running errands, preparing materials, arranging field trips, grading objective tests, and many other routine functions.

Among the first extensive programs involving teacher aides were those started in Bay City, Michigan, and Fairfield, Connecticut, in the early fifties. The movement spread slowly for a decade. The Economic Opportunity Act of 1964, the Elementary and Secondary Education Act of 1965, and the Educations Professions Act of 1967 brought about an explosive increase in the use of paraprofessionals.

Currently, about 30 per cent of the classrooms of the country have teacher aides, usually shared by two or more teachers.

Other professions, particularly medicine, have long utilized supportive personnel of many types. During the past twenty years, educators have come to the realization that routine detail work often dampens the professional teacher's enthusiasm for teaching. Trivial duties rob him of the opportunities for creative planning and decision-making that are satisfying to the professional. His skills are often diverted to performing what he considers clerical and technical chores. The public, too, is demanding that the teacher devote his time, energy, and professional competence to diagnosing the problems of children and inspiring and guiding them to excellence.

Significant Components *Which are essential?*

1. Careful planning is necessary to assure effective utilization of teacher aides.
2. The roles and duties of the professionals and paraprofessionals must be clarified.
3. Inservice training of teachers is needed to learn how to use aides to best advantage.
4. Aides should be carefully screened and trained.
5. Aides must possess ability to relate well to people and take a personal interest in children.
6. Flexibility must allow them to assume increased responsibility as they grow in confidence and competence.
7. Aides must comprehend the philosophy of the school, the objectives, the characteristics of the pupils, their own limitations, and what is expected of them.
8. Provision must be made for teachers and aides to plan together.
9. Regular attendance of the aides should be assured.
10. Parents must be assured that aides are not performing professional tasks beyond their level of competence.
11. Pupils, aides, administrators, and teachers must understand their respective roles.
12. The teacher must be glad to have an aide and to work with her.
13. Aides must be made to feel that they are important people, and that they are making a significant contribution.
14. Aides should be treated with consideration and must not be overburdened with work.
15. Aides should be recruited upon the basis of the unique needs that prevail in a particular situation.

16. Teachers must take into account the talents of the aides, their background, and their ability to relate to people.
17. The unique talents of the teacher and the aide should be matched so that they can complement each other.
18. The need for the aides must be justifiable, and the public should be informed of the reasons for employing them.
19. Employment of aides must not be an economy measure.

Proposed Advantages *With which ones do you agree?*

1. The teacher is relieved of trivia and can direct time and energy to professional services for children.
2. More and better instructional materials can be produced.
3. Students can be given more personal and individual instruction.
4. Aides bring special talents, such as proficiency in a foreign language, to the classroom.
5. More multi-media materials are likely to be utilized.
6. Aides sometimes uncover information about students that the teacher might not.
7. Additional opportunity for drill and practice reinforces what the teacher has taught.
8. Individual attention gives the pupil a feeling of importance and security.
9. Aides help to bridge the gap between home and school.
10. The presence of an adult in the room stimulates the teacher to consistently better performance.
11. Change of pace in the routine of the classroom provides an opportunity for reflection and creativity.
12. Some aides from lower-class backgrounds communicate better with some pupils than do middle-class teachers.
13. Aides are particularly helpful with handicapped, emotionally disturbed, or mentally retarded children.
14. Aides can help pupils who have been absent from school.
15. Aides provide help with remedial work; they also offer challenges to gifted pupils.
16. Often aides are more proficient and comfortable in clerical and technical areas than teachers.
17. Money is better spent because, although aides are paid less than teachers, they perform many duties as effectively.
18. The paraprofessional program utilizes untapped human resources of the community.

19. Using auxiliary personnel helps provide time for planning and curriculum revision.
20. Some aides go on to professional careers.

Criticisms and Difficulties to Be Anticipated *Do you agree?*

1. Utilizing teacher aides distorts the image of the teaching profession in the eyes of the public by making it appear that anybody can be an adequate teacher.
2. Good paraprofessionals are difficult to recruit and train.
3. The constant presence of adults tends to make children overdependent.
4. Aides from the community cannot be trusted with confidential information and records.
5. Parents are concerned about having their children under the tutelage of a noncertificated person.
6. Some teachers are uneasy with another adult in the classroom, and insecure teachers are threatened by competent paraprofessionals.
7. Many teachers are basically technicians and clerks, enjoy such work, and are reluctant to give it up.
8. If aides can do a satisfactory job, administrators and boards of education may employ them as an economy measure.
9. A teacher-aide program is likely to have a depressing effect on teacher salaries.
10. Some teachers may use aides to avoid necessary work and waste time while the aides are working with the children.
11. Teachers become jealous if they don't all have equal help from paraprofessionals.
12. Standards and the line of demarcation between instructional and noninstructional tasks have not been clearly defined.
13. Volunteer aides usually are available only a few hours per week, are undependable, and cause rapid turnover.
14. There are very few good training programs for paraprofessionals.
15. Aides become unhappy if they have too little responsibility and equally dissatisfied if they have too much.
16. If paraprofessionals become proficient, clashes between them and the teacher are likely to result.
17. Since aides are frequently established members of the community, it is difficult to get rid of them if they are troublesome.

Summary Assessment

Since World War II, the dramatic expansion of knowledge, the growing complexity of our democratic-industrial society, and the unpredictable responses of youth to the tensions and frustrations of modern living have all descended upon the classroom. On the other hand, better trained teachers have at their disposal better school buildings, better equipment, better materials, better insights into human psychology, better diagnostic tools, and better professional know-how.

The rationale for employing teacher aides usually uses the model of the medical profession. Today junior practitioners, interns, nurses, dieticians, technicians, and other supportive personnel provide many services formerly performed by expert diagnosticians and surgeons.

It appears that educators and the lay public have become convinced that supportive personnel are a good investment because they enable teachers to direct their talents to analyzing pupil needs and prescribing appropriate learning experiences. Emphasis on individualizing instruction is perhaps the most promising educational development of our time.

The value of teacher aides in multiunit schools and in team teaching situations has been convincingly demonstrated although their effectiveness varies with the different attitudes of teachers and the commitment of the school system. Some differences of opinion persist regarding assignment of paraprofessionals to duties that bring them into close contact with actual instruction. More study needs to be directed toward defining the respective roles of instructional and noninstructional personnel, assessing the effectiveness of various strategies, establishing minimum standards and criteria for selection of aides, and developing improved programs of preparation and inservice training of paraprofessionals.

The movement toward teacher aides has a brief history. However, the extent of its acceptance by an originally reluctant teaching profession and lay public and its adoption by school districts leave little doubt that it is here to stay. Teacher aides will permit the professional teacher to apply greater imagination to his work and to derive increased satisfaction from it. The program will move teaching a big step closer to achieving its hopes and potential.

A Few Leaders in the Movement

Frances P. Friedman	Harold Howe	James Olivero
John Gardner	Gayle Janowitz	Mel H. Robb

A Few Places Where the Innovation Is Used

Bay City, Mich.	Minneapolis, Minn.	San Antonio, Tex.
Cincinnati, Ohio	New Haven, Conn.	Shaker Heights, Ohio
Duluth, Minn.	Newton, Mass.	Snyder, Tex.
Fairfield, Conn.	Norwalk, Conn.	Trenton, N. J.
Huntington Beach, Calif.	St. Louis, Mo.	Washington, D. C.

Bibliography

Arcement, Sr. Genevieve, D.C., "A Teacher Aide Program That Really Works," *Catholic School Journal*, LXIX, No. 10 (1969), 26-27.

Borstad, Rodney M. and John A. Dewar, "The Paraprofessional and the States," *The National Elementary School Principal*, XLIX, No. 5 (1970), 63-67.

Bosley, Howard E., *Teacher Education In Transition*, pp. 321-331. Baltimore: Multi-State Teacher Education Project, 1969.

Caplin, Morris D., "An Invaluable Resource: The School Volunteer," *The Clearing House*, XLIV, No. 1 (1970), 10-14.

Friedman, Frances P., "Teacher Aides: Their Role in the School," *Education Canada*, IX, No. 2 (1969), 2-9.

Heppner, Harry L., "Aides . . . a boon, a blessing, an 'open sesame,' " *Journal California Teachers Association*, LXV, No. 2 (1969), 39-43.

Johnson, William H., "Utilizing Teacher Aides," *The Clearing House*, XLIII, No. 4 (1967), 229-233.

Olivero, James L. and Edward G. Buffie, *Educational Manpower*. Bloomington, Ind.: Indiana University, 1970.

Robb, Mel H., *Teacher Assistants*. Columbus, Ohio: Merrill, 1969.

Street, David, ed., *Innovations In Mass Education*, pp. 177-200. New York: Wiley, 1969.

Tanner, Laurel N. and Daniel, "The Teacher Aide: A National Study of Confusion," *Education Leadership*, XXVI, No. 8 (1969), 765-769.

"Teacher Aides in the Public Schools," *N.E.A. Research Bulletin*, XLVIII, No. 1 (1970), 11-12.

U. S. Department of Health, Education, and Welfare, *Staffing For Better Schools*. Superintendent of Documents, Washington, D.C.: Government Printing Office, 1967, pp. 13-26.

Interaction Analysis 29

Definition

Applied to education, interaction analysis is a system for observing, recording, and analyzing in quantitative terms the verbal behavior of teachers and pupils as they interact in the classroom. Developed by Ned A. Flanders in 1963, it classifies direct and indirect verbal communication in 10 categories — seven of "teacher talk," two of "student talk," and one entitled "silence or confusion." The qualitative aspects are quantified to facilitate analysis. Interaction analysis is based on the premise that the verbal behavior patterns of teachers and pupils in the classroom are significantly related to teaching effectiveness.

Verbal behavior of the teacher is tallied according to the appropriate categories and then recorded on a grid, which more easily permits interpretation. Influence which tends to limit the pupil's choice of response is classified as "direct," and that which tends to increase the student's freedom of response as "indirect." In the Flanders system, verbal behavior is coded at three-second intervals. The coding may be done by a trained observer either in the classroom or from a tape recording at any subsequent time. The purpose of the coding is to quantify the data in terms of its nature and frequency so that it can be readily summarized and analyzed on an objective basis. Its specificity and objectivity provide a common ground for the teacher and the analyst to consider the teacher's directive and nondirective verbal influence. The coding should not be misconstrued as indicating that all direct behavior is bad, nor that all indirect influence is good.

Since the process involves spontaneous verbal behavior and considers only limited aspects of the teaching-learning situation, it is well suited to analysis of both preservice and inservice performance. As in microteaching, its purpose is not evaluation or rating of teachers; it is designed as a tool to provide an objective basis for analysis and subsequent improvement of instruction.

Significant Components *Which are essential?*

1. It must be understood that the purpose of the process is the improvement of teaching and learning.
2. Emphasis is shifted from direct, teacher-initiated response to indirect, student-initiated behavior.
3. The focus is placed upon positive verbal reinforcement.
4. Both cognitive and affective aspects of communication are considered.
5. Rapport and unity of purpose must be established between teacher and analyst.
6. The significance of the relationship between teacher behavior and pupil reaction must be recognized.
7. The process must be objectified so that the outcome is determined by the performance of the teacher rather than by the preconceived notions of the analyst.
8. To increase validity and reliability, provision can be made for a team of coders or a variety of systems.
9. The willingness of the teacher to be analyzed and his desire to improve his performance are essential.
10. Recognition of the inherent value of classroom give-and-take is the vital component of the system.
11. To secure observer reliability, teachers should be given training before becoming observers.
12. The administration of the school must understand the system and be supportive of it.
13. Data should not be used for administrative purposes.
14. Sufficient time should be provided for follow-up discussion between teacher and analyst.
15. Behavior must be free and spontaneous so that experimentation is encouraged.

16. Evaluator and teacher must feel that they are working together for better teaching and learning.

Proposed Advantages *With which ones do you agree?*

1. The system provides rapid feedback.
2. Interaction analysis recognizes behavioral goals by indicating specifically the criteria on which performance will be evaluated.
3. The analysis lends itself equally well to preservice and inservice improvement efforts.
4. The system accepts the ideas and performance of students and teachers.
5. Questioning is improved.
6. Teachers are stimulated to adopt creative modes of interaction following unexpected response from students.
7. Teachers are awakened to new purposes and identification of unique patterns of interaction.
8. The feedback makes teachers aware of different modes and levels of learning.
9. The process reveals discrepancies between what the teacher intends to do and what he actually does.
10. The system is a valuable tool for research because it provides objective data relating to the teaching act.
11. Interaction analysis serves as a common ground for a supervisory conference, making it objective, meaningful, and relevant.
12. The development of indirect ways of communicating with students and relating to them is promoted.
13. Giving careful attention to detail and technical skill is essential whether teaching is looked upon as an art or a science.
14. Interaction analysis is a strong motivating force for both teachers and pupils.
15. A sense of inquiry, creative thinking, and experimentation is developed.
16. The process points up the value of active participation, which helps pupils to achieve, feel successful, and develop better attitudes.
17. Interaction analysis provides definite, systematic data rarely available to a teacher regarding his performance and its influence on the behavior of the learner.
18. Self-evaluation, self-motivation, and self-improvement are stimulated.
19. The teacher's confidence in the purpose, validity, and reliability of evaluation is increased.

20. The total learning climate is improved.
21. Teachers learn to lecture only at appropriate times.
22. Interaction analysis gives direction to teacher preparation and improvement of instruction.

Criticisms and Difficulties to Be Anticipated *Do you agree?*

1. Teachers mistrust the purposes of interaction analysis because it is new and strange.
2. Judgments may be made after too few visits or too little observation.
3. The analyst may not be skilled enough to insure reliability.
4. The whole process distorts the normalcy of the teaching situation.
5. Statements or questions of teachers are difficult to fit into a classification system .
6. Teachers may try to beat the game.
7. The whole system is too complicated and unwieldy and takes too much time and effort to explain to teachers.
8. The system implies that silence and confusion are the same.
9. The process tells the teacher where he is, but makes no suggestions for improvement.
10. It neglects teaching style and many important learning activities by stressing only verbal behavior.
11. Student teachers particularly may overlook the appropriateness factor and change their performance from one type of behavior to another too soon, too often, or too rapidly.
12. Coding verbal behavior destroys the wholeness of the teaching act.
13. The system tries to make a science out of an art, disregarding the intricate nature of teaching.
14. The system overlooks the unique qualities and strengths of each teacher.
15. Too few trained observers are available.

Summary Assessment

The beginnings of the program of interaction analysis can be traced to early research by Kurt Lewin, Ronald Lippett, and Ralph White relating to autocratic, democratic, and laissez-faire leadership qualities. The Flanders system of verbal-interaction analysis is the best known and most widely used. Others, however, are being developed. Some of them are merely modifications or adaptations of the Flanders technique and limit themselves to verbal behavior. Others, using the same general approach, propose to incorporate more aspects of the teacher's performance. The OScAR V4 (Observation Schedule and Record 4, Verbal), for example, considers the time a teacher spends in management and instruction. Charles Galloway's work with nonverbal interaction is gaining recognition as a tool for studying another significant aspect of the teaching act.

Although research evidence of its value is not conclusive, interaction analysis has proved itself as a method for gathering one type of objective data and summarizing it. It has established itself as a good tool for diagnosis and improvement. It has also called attention to the relationship between what a teacher does and the influence his performance has upon learners. Those who are concerned about the fact that the Flanders system considers only verbal behavior fail to recognize that that is all it proposes to analyze. Then, too, verbal communication has been, and is likely to continue to be, a very important aspect of almost all teaching and learning.

Interaction analysis contributes significantly to identification of verbal behavior patterns that affect learning both positively and negatively. It helps teachers and supervisors in analyzing performance and in planning appropriate behavioral changes.

Although to date it has been used mainly with student teachers, the concept is gaining broader acceptance. The approach is likely to spread to include many aspects of teaching other than verbal interaction. Its use will increase in both the preservice and inservice training of school personnel, and its value will become more significant in research and supervision as teaching continues to mature as a profession.

A Few Leaders in the Movement

Edmund J. Amidon
Joseph C. Bondi
C. T. Campbell
Ned A. Flanders
Charles M. Galloway
Joseph B. Hough
Philip Jackson
Richard L. Ober
John Withall

A Few Places Where the Innovation Is Used

Appalachia Ed. Lab.
Claremont, Calif.
Marywood College
Miami Univ.
Ohio State Univ.
Pa. State Univ.
Provo, Utah
St. Martin's College
Temple Univ.
Univ. of Fla.
Univ. of Mich.
Univ. of N. H.
Univ. of South Fla.
Univ. of Wis.
Whitman College

Bibliography

Allen, Paul M. et al., *Teacher Self-Appraisal: A Way of Looking Over Your Own Shoulder*. Worthington, Ohio: Charles A. Jones, 1970.

Amidon, Edmund J. and Ned A. Flanders, *The Role of the Teacher in the Classroom*. Minneapolis, Minn.: Association for Productive Teaching, 1967.

Amidon, Edmund and John H. Hough, eds., *Interaction Analysis: Theory Research and Application*. Reading, Mass.: Addison-Wesley, 1967.

Amidon, Edmund and Elizabeth Hunter, *Improving Teaching—The Analysis of Classroom Verbal Interaction*. New York: Holt, 1966.

Biddle, Bruce J. and William J. Ellena, eds., *Contemporary Research on Teacher Effectivness*, pp. 196-231. New York: Holt, 1964.

Bondi, Joseph C., Jr., "The Effects of Interaction Analysis Feedback on the Verbal Behavior of Student Teachers," *Educational Leadership*, XXVI, No. 8 (1969), 794-799.

———, "Feedback from Interaction Analysis: Some Implications for the Improvement of Teaching," *The Journal of Teacher Education*, XXI, No. 2 (1970), 189-96.

Flanders, Ned A., *Analyzing Teacher Behavior*. Reading, Mass.: Addison-Wesley, 1970.

French, Russell L. and Charles M. Galloway, "A New Look at Classroom Interactions," *Educational Leadership*, XXVII, No. 6 (1970), 548-552.

Hough, John B., Ernest E. Lohman, and Richard Ober, "Shaping and Predicting Verbal Teaching Behavior in a General Methods Course," *The Journal of Teacher Education*, XX, No. 2 (1969), 213-224.

Mager, Robert F., *Developing Attitude Toward Learning*. Palo Alto, Calif.: Fearon, 1968.

Minnis, Douglas, "Interacting in the Interrogative," *Journal of Teacher Education*, XX, No. 4 (1969), 201-212.

Ober, Richard L., "The Nature of Interaction Analysis," *High School Journal*, LI, No. 1 (1967), 7-16.

Pickett, Laurel Anne, "Can the Level of Instruction Be Raised Through the Use of Interaction Analysis?" *Education Leadership*, XXVII, No. 6 (1970), 597-600.

Psencik, Leroy F., "Interaction Analysis Improves Classroom Instruction," *The Clearing House*, XLIII, No. 9 (1969), 555-560.

Queen, Bernarde and Phil E. Suiter, *Interaction Analysis—A Self Instructional Program for Teachers*. Charleston, W. Va.: Appalachia Educational Lab., 1968.

Shrable, Kenneth and Douglas Minnis, "Interacting in the Interrogative," *Journal of Teacher Education*, XX, No. 2 (1969), 201-211.

Microteaching 30

Definition

Microteaching is a teacher-training and improvement technique developed at Stanford University in the early sixties. Although video taping is not a requirement, microteaching commonly involves video taping a short lesson, usually of five- to ten-minute duration, playing it back, making a critique of it, and repeating the operation to improve certain components of the microlesson. It is used principally in the preservice education of teachers, for the improvement of teachers in service, and for research involving the study of the teaching and learning process. The number of students involved is small, usually four to six.

For these purposes, microteaching has advantages over regular teaching in that the analysis of the performance is based upon incidents and acts that are specific and can be replayed. Many of the constraints of the normal classroom can be eliminated, and controlled conditions can be developed. The performance can be observed by the teacher himself or by him and his supervisor or colleagues. The feedback is real and rapid. A record is made so that an original teaching performance can be kept for comparison with refinements in subsequent reteaching. At the reteaching stage, it is often more interesting and beneficial to focus on the same techniques applied in a fresh lesson rather than a repeat of the old one.

By reducing the usual complexities involved in the classroom, attention can be focused upon a limited number of techniques. Feedback is obtained from the video tape, the reaction of students, the teacher's own observation and analysis, and the suggestions of other observers such as supervisors. The review makes immediate and individual diagnosis possible and suggests ways of improving. Reteaching can take place immediately after the review and critical analysis of the microlesson or at any subsequent time.

Significant Components *Which are essential?*

1. The purposes of the microlesson must be clearly understood, and the technique defined in behavioral terms.
2. Careful and detailed planning is essential.
3. Only supervisors, teacher-education instructors, and fellow teachers with positive, helpful attitudes and manners can be effective in microteaching.
4. The trainee must feel free from threat so that he is willing and ready to experiment and accept criticism.
5. Microteaching should be looked upon as a valuable aid to improving competencies, not as a complete program.
6. Lessons must be considered as bases for diagnosis and refinement rather than models of perfection.
7. Skilled and experienced supervisors are an advantage.
8. Trust and respect between teacher and evaluator is essential for open and constructive criticism.
9. Time devoted to practice must depend upon the problems under consideration, the needs of the trainees, and their levels of competence.
10. Utilization of microteaching for research should be built into the total program.
11. The trainee must be able to describe precisely the skill under study, know for what purpose it is to be used, recognize it when he sees it, and know when and under what conditions it is appropriate.

Proposed Advantages *With which ones do you agree?*

1. Microteaching shifts attention from generalized competencies to specific behavioral acts of the teacher.
2. Microteaching is equally effective for training teachers initially, for improving the skills of experienced teachers, and for enhancing the performance of supervisors.

3. Analysis of the subject matter, the performance of the teacher, reaction of students, and appropriateness of various activities can be studied in microteaching.
4. The record that is preserved allows different people to observe the performance and make a critique of it at different times.
5. When desired, alterations can readily be made in the various components.
6. Comments of the supervisor are definite, understandable, and relevant because they pertain to precise acts.
7. The system can be used for improving all aspects of teaching, from grooming to intricate matters of teacher-student interaction.
8. In the preservice program, microteaching relieves many of the tensions experienced by the neophyte when he confronts a large class in his first experience.
9. By giving a trainee and supervisor a chance to talk alone, the process reduces the embarrassment common in classroom supervision.
10. Microteaching takes less time than traditional student teaching to produce comparable results.
11. The system can be used in any college course, including those designed for the preparation of supervisors and administrators.
12. The teacher can see if his strategies and techniques are doing what he wants them to do.
13. Microteaching makes the trainee sensitive to both verbal and nonverbal behavior and to the fact that improvement requires careful reflection and continuous refinement.
14. For research purposes, the microlesson can reduce the range of factors in the teaching-learning situation, readily manipulate variables, and keep factors extraneous to the techniques at a minimum.
15. Microteaching quickens the preservice student's interest in being a teacher and stimulates the experienced teacher's desire for self-improvement by making the improvement process enjoyable and observable.
16. By comparing subsequent performances with earlier ones, the process vividly portrays growth in skill and develops confidence.
17. The specificity of microteaching enables the teacher to develop concrete ways of implementing such generalizations as "making the lesson more interesting," "demonstrating greater enthusiasm," or "motivating the student."
18. A supervisor who works together with a teacher in analyzing specific performance and making definite suggestions is likely to be fair and helpful.

19. The supervisor will grow in his skill in identifying and improving important components of teaching.

Criticisms and Difficulties to Be Anticipated *Do you agree?*

1. Microteaching conveys the impression that the teacher, rather than the student, is the important figure in the lesson.
2. Microteaching is artificial because it eliminates many of the complexities of teaching in the classroom.
3. The short lesson may not fit in naturally, be representative of the activities of a longer period, or be long enough to illustrate many valuable strategies.
4. Supervisors may be overcritical.
5. Continuous concentration on small segments of a lesson and on precise behavior destroys the art of teaching.
6. The small group of students in the class do not put skills and techniques to a real test.
7. The process focuses attention on such factors as grooming, gestures, and voice rather than on more important aspects of teaching, such as pupil-teacher interaction.
8. The outward appearance of skills and techniques may overshadow their appropriateness and inherent value.
9. Equipment is costly, required supervisory time is excessive, and it is difficult to secure students.
10. There are so many things that can go wrong with schedules, persons, and equipment.
11. Trainees, especially teachers in service, may be resistant to participating.
12. Inadequate organization and administration render microteaching ineffective.
13. Little opportunity is provided for experiencing the normal flow of activities that exists in the regular classroom as students move from one learning experience to another.

Summary Assessment

Because of its adaptability, its provision for feedback and re-use, and its focus on specific acts and skills, microteaching has generated great interest on the part of trainees and supervisors. By reducing the complexities of the typical classroom, the teaching-learning environment can be manipulated by the process to direct attention to a limited number of specific techniques. This focus is helpful to both teacher and student. Because the procedure promotes learning through involvement, reflection, and self-evaluation, it provides unusual opportunity for improvement in teacher competence. Showing him how he has performed is strong motivation for the trainee. Yet the situation is somewhat artificial since few regular classrooms resemble the microteaching model.

Although microteaching has not been without problems, it has had great appeal and promises to become even more popular and valuable as its processes are refined. Students in preparation for teaching, teachers in service, college instructors, supervisory personnel, and researchers are becoming increasingly aware of its motivational power and its potentialities for producing changes in instructional behavior.

As they come to realize that microteaching is basically a strategy for improving teaching and learning, not for rating teachers, educators will feel less threatened and be less threatening about participating in recorded performances, and in systematic evaluation of them. Innovations in goals, methods, and materials give experienced teachers a feeling of need for lifelong improvement. Microteaching makes continuous growth in proficiency attractive and exciting by providing a vehicle for cooperative effort among all those engaged in the educational enterprise. It is likely to be used more extensively for research, for improvement of college instruction, for training of supervisory personnel, and for enhancing learning opportunities for children. Its future looks bright.

A Few Leaders in the Movement

Keith Acheson
Dwight W. Allen
W. R. Borg
Robert N. Bush
Jimmie C. Fortune
W. Warren Kallenbach
James Olivero
Michael E. J. Orme
Kevin Ryan
Al Seagren
Thomas Stroud
David B. Young

A Few Places Where the Innovation Is Used

Brigham Young Univ.
Chicago, Ill.
Detroit, Mich.
Hainesville, Ga.
Howard County, Md.
Jefferson County, Colo.
Johns Hopkins Univ.
Stanford Univ.
N. M. State Univ.
Northeast La. College
St. Marys Dom. College
Univ. of Ill.
Univ. of Md.
Univ. of Mass.
Vanderbilt Univ.

Bibliography

Adams, Raymond S. and Bruce J. Biddle, *Realities of Teaching-Explorations With Video Tape*. New York: Holt, 1970.

Allen, Dwight, "Microteaching: A New Framework for In-Service Education," *The High School Journal*, XLIX, No. 8 (1966), 355-362.

Allen, Dwight and Kevin Ryan, *Microteaching*. Reading, Mass.: Addison-Wesley, 1969.

Bosley, Howard E., *Teacher Education In Transition*, pp. 249-261. Baltimore: Multi-State Teacher Education Project, 1969.

———, *Teacher Education In Transition, Volume II, Emerging Roles and Responsibilities*, pp. 121-150. Baltimore: Multi-State Teacher Education Project, 1969.

Edelfelt, Roy A., ed., *Innovative Programs In Student Teaching*. Baltimore: Maryland State Department of Education, 1969.

Fortune, Jimmie C., James M. Cooper, and Dwight Allen, "The Stanford Summer Microteaching Clinic, 1965," *Journal of Teacher Education*, XVIII, No. 4 (1967), 389-393.

Gardner, Marjorie and Rolland Bartholomew, "Microteaching," *Science Teacher*, XXXVI, No. 5 (1969), 45-47.

Kallenbach, W. Warren, "The Effectiveness of Microteaching in the Preparation of Elementary Intern Teachers," AERA Paper Abstracts, Washington, D.C.: *American Educational Research Association*, 1968.

Kallenbach, W. Warren and Meredith D. Gall, "Microteaching Versus Conventional Methods in Training Elementary Intern Teachers," *The Journal of Educational Research*, LXIII, No. 3 (1969), 136-141.

Langer, Philip, "Minicourse: Theory and Strategy," *Educational Technology*, IX, No. 9 (1969), 54-59.

McCollum, Robert and Donald La Due, "Microteaching in a Teacher Education Program," *Social Education*, XXXIV, No. 3 (1970), 333-336.

Olivero, James, *Microteaching: Medium for Improving Instruction*. Columbus, Ohio: Merrill, 1970.

"Teaching Teachers," *National Elementary Principal*, XLVIII, No. 4 (1969), 30-31.

Young, David B., "The Modification of Teacher Behavior Using Video-Taped Models in a Microteaching Sequence," *Educational Leadership*, XXVI, No. 4 (1969), 394-403.

Young, David B. and Dorothy A. Young, "The Model in Use," *Theory Into Practice*, VII (1968), 186-189.

Index